THE BEAC

G000166087

Copyright © 1997 Omnibus Press
(A Division of Book Sales Limited)

Edited by Chris Charlesworth
Cover & Book designed by 4i Limited
Picture research by Nikki Russell

ISBN 0.7119.5595.6 Order No.OP47827

Exclusive Distributors
Book Sales Limited, 8/9 Frith Street, London W1V 5TZ, UK.
Music Sales Corporation, 257 Park Avenue South, New York, NY 10010, USA.
Music Sales Pty Limited, 120 Rothschild Avenue, Rosebery, NSW 2018, Australia.

To the Music Trade only
Music Sales Limited, 8/9 Frith Street, London W1V 5TZ, UK.

Photo credits: Front cover: Harry Goodwin; all other pictures supplied by Harry Goodwin, LFI and Barry Plummer.
Every effort has been made to trace the copyright holders of the photographs in this book but one or two were unreachable. We would be
grateful if the photographers concerned would contact us.

Printed in the United Kingdom by Ebenzer Baylis & Son, Worcester.

A catalogue record for this book is available from the British Library.

OMNIBUS PRESS
LONDON · NEW YORK · SYDNEY

CONTENTS

INTRODUCTION

It was the late Dennis Wilson who, with his usual verbal economy, offered that "Brian Wilson is The Beach Boys. We're just his messengers. He's everything – we're nothing".

It all began some 35 years ago, over the 1961 September Labor Day weekend, when three brothers, a cousin and a high school buddy took advantage of parental absence, and unwittingly embarked on an All-American saga that shows few signs of ending, has seen all possible shades of light and darkness (even death), and, most importantly, has gifted us a legacy of some of the most exciting, uplifting and emotionally affecting music of the rock era. Before 1967, the story of The Beach Boys was an apparently inexorable rise to international stardom, embracing and discarding such fads as surfing and hot-rods as Brian's musical genius expanded from the initial shock of 'Surfin' USA' to the complex tapestry of 'Good Vibrations'; perhaps the only slight stutter along the way was the less than ecstatic reaction of the American public to the now rightfully acclaimed 'Pet Sounds'. The non-release of the legendary 'Smile' album proved a brutally abrupt end to the golden era.

The post-'Smile' years saw the band manfully soldiering on – and occasionally triumphing – in the face of the increasing absence of their guiding light, as Brian Wilson gradually withdrew from normal life, a victim of alarming drug abuse, his considerable insecurity, family pressures and, perhaps most tellingly, his own expectations. It wasn't until the late Seventies that he began to rebuild his life and career, and not until the Nineties that he truly became his own man again. The Beach Boys, apparently by default, have chosen an easier path since the late Seventies, largely abandoning the studio for the concert stage, content to reprise a string of hits older than a large proportion of their audience.

These days, it's hard to believe that this was the band who not only survived the so-called British invasion of the USA but fought back to such effect that for a period of some months (late 1966-early 1967), The Beach Boys, and in particular Brian Wilson, were considered at least the musical equals of the Fab Four; it's equally hard to appreciate that by refusing to record in their Company's studios, this was the band who effectively freed the music industry from such restrictive practices. It is also hard to recall that their own Brother Records predated Apple by a good year, an innovation usually obscured by the label's swift demise. To see the surviving members still going through the motions on stage for the umpteenth time is like watching a bad print of a classic silent movie – the original glory dimmed by time, often only hinted at... but it's still good to have them around at all.

Rock music is still evolving: only now can a truly objective view of the birth of the movement in the Fifties be considered. Thus for now the view that The Beatles dominated the Sixties to the exclusion of every other white band still prevails... but in another hundred years or so, it's entirely possible that the opinion of one noted Beach Boys historian might prevail: "Sure, The Beatles will be remembered, and rightly so, as the sociological phenomenon of the Sixties... but if you're talking about music, it has to be Brian Wilson & The Beach Boys. That's who they'll be studying."

The authors would like to express their appreciation to the following, without whose invaluable assistance (directly or indirectly), this project would have been that much more arduous: extra-special thanks to David Leaf, Domenic Priore and Brad Elliott (devoted historians and excellent scribes to a man, whose writings are as entertaining as they are essential); special thanks also to Mike Grant, Chris White and the staff of Beach Boys Stomp; Peter Reum; Rick Smith; Stephen McParland; Bill Scanlan-Murphy; Kingsley Abbott; Peter Doggett; Lynda Morrison; Chris Charlesworth; Pete Frame; Ray McCarthy; Harold Bronson; Bernard Doherty; Timothy White; Byron Preiss, and the surviving Beach Boys, especially BW...

For current information on Brian Wilson & The Beach Boys, you'd be well advised to subscribe to the following publications (for details send an SAE/IRC):
UK Europe: Beach Boys Stomp, 22 Avondale Road, Wealdstone, Middlesex HA3 7RE
USA: Endless Summer Quarterly, PO Box 470315, Charlotte, NC 28247

The current availability of Beach Boys albums on CD is, considering their importance to the history of rock'n'roll, scandalous. In 1990, the award-winning Capitol reissue programme was a fan's dream come true; excepting 'Pet Sounds' and the 'Christmas Album', repackaged singly, all the band's non-compilation Capitol albums were reissued, superbly remastered, in a two-LPs-on-one-CD format (hence the "Twofer" handle) at mid-price, complete with bonus tracks (either non-LP singles or previously unreleased material from the period) and excellent (and extensive) booklets written by expert Beach Boys commentator and Brian Wilson biographer David Leaf (currently Wilson's personal manager).

The reissue of the Warners and CBS material (by Sony) in 1991 was less elaborate (no notes, no bonus cuts); nonetheless, by the end of that year, just about every original Beach Boys album released between 1962-1989 could be found on CD. Since then, with the exception of 'Pet Sounds', all the Capitol Twofers and the Sony CDs have been deleted. Reverting to type, Capitol have since reissued (in the USA only) the Twofers as single CDs, minus the booklets and bonus tracks (raising suspicions of a 'bonus tracks only' CD in the future). Capitol also own the CBS material, and it has been mooted that the post-Sixties albums may one day be re-reissued with notes and bonus tracks.

Stop press news is that May, 1996, was supposedly the scheduled release date of a 30th anniversary 4 CD 'Pet Sounds' boxed set, comprising session material, instrumental backing tracks, isolated vocal tracks, a new re-mastered mono version of the album, and a first ever true stereo mix. Perhaps predictably, apparently inevitable objections from the group have delayed release until late 1996/early 1997.

Andrew G. Doe & John Tobler, March, 1996

SURFIN' SAFARI

(CAPITOL T-1808 [LP], CDP 7 93691 2 [CD]; RELEASED OCTOBER, 1962)

Rebuffed by the vast majority of labels in Los Angeles, despite the local chart success of their début single, 'Surfin'', The Beach Boys signed to Capitol Records in summer, 1962, beginning a seven year working relationship that would span 16 original LPs, eventually disintegrate in mutual acrimony and litigation... and establish the band as the foremost American group of the early Sixties, the only ones to successfully challenge – and briefly usurp – the supremacy of another band whose name also begins with B-E-A. However, 'Surfin' Safari' displays little, if any, of the potential of The Beach Boys; this is a band growing up before your very ears. Mike Love, the eldest, was barely 21, Brian Wilson, a year younger, and all – bar Brian on keyboards and his brother Carl, on guitar – were still learning their instruments.

Although the album was "officially" produced by Capitol A&R man Nik Venet, informed opinion suggests that Brian Wilson was actually calling the shots, except on the songs taken from the demo sent to Capitol, which were produced by his father – and then band manager – Murry Wilson. While 'Surfin' Safari' is a far less auspicious début LP than, say, 'Please Please Me' or 'The Doors', it's not without interest (as the début of a major group), and even charm (albeit rather dated); at worst, it provides a benchmark against which all later releases (and non-releases...) may be judged. It spent nearly 40 weeks in the US LP chart, just missing the Top 30. No true stereo version of this album has ever been released (nor is one known to even exist, although the bonus CD track, 'Land Ahoy', allows for such a possibility). The band as pictured on the sleeve includes David Marks, a neighbour of the Wilson family and friend of Carl's; Marks temporarily replaced Alan Jardine when the latter saw a more secure and remunerative future in dentistry and departed prior to the Capitol contract. Unless otherwise specified, the lead vocalist throughout was Mike Love.

(NB: where Love's composer credit is followed by *, these songs were decreed by a 1994 Los Angeles court decision to have been co-written by him, although he was never previously credited as such; the bonus tracks included on Capitol's 1990 CD reissue programme are noted by +.)

SURFIN' SAFARI
(B.Wilson/Love)

One of three tracks to feature Alan Jardine, this re-recording of a song originally cut during the Hite Morgan sessions of September/October 1961 (see Lost & Found below) featured on a five-song demo tape submitted by Murry Wilson to Capitol. A logical follow-on from 'Surfin'' and a Top 20 hit, it apparently wasn't the designated A-side of the first Capitol 45, but as it was making waves in such unlikely spots as distinctly landlocked Phoenix, Arizona, it was repromoted as the main event. The lyrics are notably different from the original, and the session that produced this title (and the rest of the demo) marked Brian Wilson's first association with Western Studios and more importantly, with

engineer Chuck Britz, who went on to work the board on almost every Beach Boys hit before 1967.

COUNTY FAIR
(B.Wilson/Usher)

Gary Usher, the nephew of a neighbour of the Wilsons, was Brian's first musical collaborator outside the band, eventually falling foul of manager Murry's suspicious nature. Written in ten minutes, 'County Fair' was later reworked by Brian as 'I Do', which he produced for The Castells. Mike Love apparently supplied the barker's spiel.

TEN LITTLE INDIANS
(B.Wilson/Usher)

Figuring that the surfin' craze was dead, Capitol chose this as the second Beach Boys single, which just went Top 50 to become their smallest US hit for the next six years. Nonetheless, the vocal arrangement on the chorus still catches the ear.

CHUG-A-LUG
(B.Wilson/Usher/Love*)

Interesting mainly for its thumbnail sketches of the band members and friends ("Dennis (Wilson) wonders what's under the hood...") and an organ break by Brian Wilson.

LITTLE GIRL (YOU'RE MY MISS AMERICA)
(Catalano/Alpert)

That's Alpert as in Herb, co-founder with Jerry Moss of A&M Records. Dennis Wilson's first lead vocal.

409
(B.Wilson/Usher/Love*)

Another song from the Murry Wilson-produced demo tape (and thus featuring Alan Jardine), and allegedly the original A-side of the first Capitol 45, '409' stemmed from Usher's burning desire to own a 409 Chevrolet, in 1961 the car to drive. Ironically, the engine sounds – taped early in the morning outside the Wilson house in Hawthorne, a Los Angeles suburb – are of Usher's 348 Chevy !

SURFIN'
(B.Wilson/Love)

The first ever Beach Boys 45, produced by and leased from Hite Morgan (and not, as long supposed, a re-recording), was inspired by Dennis Wilson, the only true surfer in the band, who provided Love with the jargon to fit to Brian Wilson's music. The band for this recording comprised Mike Love (lead vocals), Dennis Wilson (vocals), Carl Wilson (guitar, vocals), Alan Jardine (acoustic bass, vocals) and Brian Wilson (vocals, percussion). If the track sounds unnatural, it's because Murry Wilson mastered it at above-normal tape speed to make the band sound "youthful". The single was a big local hit but made only a minimal impression on the national chart, peaking below #70. Included on the 1993 boxed set was the earliest known Beach Boys recording, a rehearsal session for 'Surfin'' taped (presumably) at the Wilson house.

SUMMERTIME BLUES
(Cochran/Capehart)

Did any emergent band in the early/mid-Sixties *not* feature this classic Eddie Cochran saga of teenage angst in its stage act? Lead vocal shared between Love and Brian Wilson, but an uninspired cover.

CUCKOO CLOCK
(B.Wilson/Usher)

With the chorus apparently a reference to Murry's pet mynah bird, this isn't one of Brian Wilson's better vocals. The Hammond organ break promises later and greater things...

MOON DAWG
(Weaver)

Carl Wilson's first attempt at guitar heroics. Derry Weaver is actually producer Nik Venet, who also supplies the howls and barks. Perhaps the earliest glimpse of the most fabled block harmonies in the world, and with a shockingly obvious edit!

HEADS YOU WIN, TAILS I LOSE
(B.Wilson/Usher)

The least discerning musical ear will realise that Dennis Wilson's drumming was basic – "I'm a clubber, not a drummer", he once offered.

THE SHIFT
(B.Wilson/Love)

An ode not to gear sticks, but to current beach fashions... and a melody similar to 'Shut Down'.

CINDY, OH CINDY+
(Barons/Long)

Recorded after the album sessions, the first voice heard is that of Murry Wilson, while the lead vocal is by Brian Wilson. This abysmal sped-up version of the 1956 US hit for both Vince Martin & The Tarriers and Eddie Fisher should have remained "in the can".

LAND AHOY+
(B.Wilson)

This album outtake (in stereo!) briefly appeared on the 1983 'Rarities' compilation (see below) of rare and unreleased Capitol cuts, which was swiftly withdrawn after legal threats from The Beach Boys. Brian Wilson recycled the melody a year later for 'Cherry, Cherry Coupe'.

SURFIN' USA
(CAPITOL ST-L890 [LP] CDP 7 93691 2 [CD]; RELEASED MARCH, 1963)

Although not recognised as such until many years later, 'Surfin' USA' was a revolutionary album, in that a band signed to a major record label for the first time demanded, and won, the right to record in the studio of their (or rather Brian Wilson's) choice, Western Recorders. Musically, however, it was a strange progression from 'Surfin' Safari', for five of the 12 cuts were instrumentals, a percentage never equalled on another Beach Boys album. Fortunately, the remaining tracks were largely strong enough to carry such dead weight, and the LP went a long way to establishing the band as a national force, and vocal surf music as a valid genre. Just missing #1, it spent 18 months on the US LP chart, and was both the first Beach Boys LP to be certified gold, and their UK album chart début in 1965, when it made the Top 20.

Although issued in both mono and stereo formats, Brian Wilson (being unable to hear in stereo due to total deafness in his right ear) personally mixed only the mono version. Any stereo mix of Beach Boys material prior to 1968 was the work of studio engineers (usually Chuck Britz). The CD mix is stereo, except for the bonus track.

SURFIN' USA
(Berry/B.Wilson)

The album's standout track, the band's finest outing thus far, a US Top 3 single, their UK chart début (not quite Top 30) and still a concert staple, 'Surfin' USA' had its origin in Brian Wilson's notion of putting surf lyrics to 'Sweet Little Sixteen'. His then-girlfriend's brother, Jimmy Bowles, supplied a list of surfing spots... and the rest is history. Early pressings of the label credited Wilson as sole composer, but Chuck Berry and his lawyers took a dim view of that, and for many years thereafter, the label credit read "Berry"!

The double tracking on Love's lead vocal – a practice used extensively hereafter – helped remove a nasal edge, and also fills out the backing vocals to great effect on what is, essentially, the first "real" Beach Boys song. When Jan & Dean visited a Beach Boys ses-

sion, Brian played them 'USA', but declined to let them record it, offering them 'Surf City' instead – thus giving away his first #1. Murry Wilson, his father, never really forgave him. The 1993 boxed set opens with a highly evocative home demo of this song – just Brian, his piano and a great idea. (Also included in the box is a storming 1964 live version, left over from the 'Beach Boys Concert' LP).

FARMER'S DAUGHTER
(B.Wilson/Love*)

A sublime Brian Wilson lead vocal, the best block harmonies to date and a spartan production make for a typical early offering. Covered, and drenched in velvet harmonies by Fleetwood Mac as an extra track on their live album in 1980.

MISIRLOU
(Dale)

"King of the Surf Guitar" Dick Dale commanded far more credibility among *real* surfers than The Beach Boys ever could (they were seen as flatlanders at best, gremmies at worst) but Dale's legendary live act rarely survived the transfer to vinyl. Probably more people have heard this version of what is regarded as a surf instrumental classic than the far superior original.

STOKED
(B.Wilson)

One of Brian Wilson's few attempts at a true surf instrumental. A brave stab.

LONELY SEA
(Usher/B.Wilson)

The unfortunate spoken section aside, this ballad – especially Brian Wilson's mournful lead vocal – was a pointer to the more personal, introspective and wistful material of the mid-Sixties.

SHUT DOWN
(B.Wilson/Christian)

The B-side of 'Surfin' USA', and a Top 30 hit in its own right, 'Shut Down' was Brian Wilson's first released collaboration with Roger Christian, a DJ whom Murry Wilson contacted after hearing him discussing '409' on his late night show – one of Murry's better ideas, as it turned out. On the mono version of the album (and the single), Love's poorly double-tracked vocal renders part of the third verse unintelligible. Love also supplies the two-note sax solo.

NOBLE SURFER
(B.Wilson/Love*)

Slightly risqué then (for the "noble/no bull" wordplay), the first verse features what was to become a Beach Boys trademark – mob-handed vocals to grab the attention. The celeste (?) break may be unique in rock'n'roll.

HONKY TONK
(Doggett)

A massive US hit for black organist Bill Doggett in 1956, and maybe the first rock'n'roll instrumental smash, is taken here at a measured stroll.

LANA
(B.Wilson)

A product of one of the first Western sessions, its writer's falsetto is well to the fore on a slightly under-developed track. A glockenspiel buried deep in the mix hints at his growing interest in unusual instrumentation.

SURF JAM
(C.Wilson)

The fourth instrumental showcases Carl Wilson's developing guitar prowess; his first

tutor was neighbour John Maus, later to find fame in The Walker Brothers.

LET'S GO TRIPPIN'
(Dale)

Another Dick Dale classic, tackled with a fair degree of gusto.

FINDERS KEEPERS
(B.Wilson/Love*)

A welcome relief after two instrumentals, this boasts not only an unusual three part structure, but also a nod towards the East Coast equivalent of The Beach Boys, The Four Seasons. Another Love double tracking disaster.

THE BAKER MAN+
(B.Wilson)

Recorded just after the LP sessions, reportedly as a publishing demo, this 'Hully Gully' derived item was unreleased until the Capitol Twofer reissue series. An unusually gritty vocal from Brian Wilson.

SURFER GIRL
(CAPITOL ST-1981 [LP] CDP 7 93692 2 [CD]; RELEASED SEPTEMBER 1963)

With this release, The Beach Boys completed their apprenticeship, delivering their first truly satisfying album, not to mention the first officially produced by Brian Wilson, a public recognition by Capitol of what many already suspected – that he was something more than a kid who could dash off a hit. It also marked another, far more significant, milestone in the band's history (and its leader's musical development) – the use of "outside" musicians.

Although Dennis Wilson drummed on the original 'Little Deuce Coupe' session, Brian had come to realise that his style and expertise were no longer sufficient, and drafted in stellar sideman Hal Blaine to supply the required precision (although Blaine himself has stated that Brian's use of session musicians began soon after 'Surfin' Safari'…). Despite his brother's misgivings, Dennis accepted the situation with equanimity, and from then on, the use of session players inexorably accelerated, the following names forming the core of Brian's trusted sidemen (and

woman): drums – Hal Blaine & Jim Gordon; percussion – Gene Estes, Julius Wechter & Frankie Capp; bass – Lyle Ritz, Carol Kaye & Ray Pohlman; guitars – Glen Campbell, Tommy Tedesco, Jerry Cole, Barney Kessell, Bill Pitman, Billy Strange, Pohlman & Kaye; horns – Steve Douglas, Jay Migliori, Roy Caton & Lou Blackburn; harmonica – Tommy Morgan; accordion – Carl Fortina & Frank Marocco; keyboards – Leon Russell, Don Randi, Larry Knechtal & Al de Lory. The majority of these excellent musicians were members of Phil Spector's famed "Wrecking Crew".

Personnel moves were also afoot: Brian was an infrequent – and increasingly unwilling – touring member, so to ease matters, Alan Jardine was recalled, and for several weeks (at least in the studio) the band numbered six… but numbered also were the days of David Marks, who never saw eye to eye with manager Murry Wilson. Accordingly, in late August, 1963, Marks was shown the door, and thus this LP became the last Beach Boys album he played on (he never sang on a Beach Boys track). This US Top 10/UK Top 20 LP went gold during over a year in the US chart.

SURFER GIRL
(B.Wilson)

The first song that Brian Wilson ever wrote – acknowledged by him as inspired by 'When You Wish Upon A Star' from the classic Disney cartoon, *Pinocchio* – and one of his sweetest-ever ballads, which remains a concert highlight. A sweeping falsetto from Brian, a universal theme and fulsome harmonies propelled the 45 into the US Top 10. Long thought to be about his first serious girlfriend, Judy Bowles, Wilson later maintained that the song (first recorded during the 1961 Morgan sessions) was written with no one specific in mind. The 'Good Vibrations' boxed set includes two 'new' live versions of this song; a wobbly outtake from the 'Concert!' album... and a somewhat stoned rendering from rehearsals in Hawaii for an unreleased live album in 1967.

CATCH A WAVE
(B.Wilson/Love*)

An arresting vocal grabber of an intro, a rotated lead vocal (Dennis Wilson – Brian Wilson – Love) and an unexpected harp glis-

sando (by Love's sister, Maureen) go a long way to making this an early Beach Boys highlight. Surf music cohorts Jan & Dean later reworked the lyric and had a huge hit with the skateboarding anthem, 'Sidewalk Surfin''.

THE SURFER MOON
(B.Wilson)

A re-recording of one of Brian Wilson's earliest – though *not* his first, as is often stated – extra-BB productions (for his then room-mate Bob Norburg), this could be his first solo effort: all the voices sound similar, and allowing for the first-ever string arrangement on a Beach Boys track, and precise drumming, this is a near certainty.

SOUTH BAY SURFER
(Foster/B.Wilson/
D.Wilson/A.Jardine)

This less than reverential reworking of Stephen Foster's 'Way Down Upon The Swanee River' is nevertheless amusing; Love and Brian Wilson share the vocals.

THE ROCKING SURFER
(Trad. arr. B.Wilson)

Another instrumental, originally tagged 'Good Humor Man' (after the American ice cream); Carl and Brian Wilson trade licks to reasonable effect.

LITTLE DEUCE COUPE
(B.Wilson/Christian)

The B-side of the 'Surfer Girl' 45, this also made the Top 20 on its own, and introduced the basic backbeat which, over the next few years (and sporadically in the Seventies) formed the foundation of many Beach Boys classics. Love had apparently mastered double tracking... and the "pink slip", a phrase which baffled many at the time, refers to the car's ownership document, then printed on (surprise!) pink paper.

IN MY ROOM
(B.Wilson/Usher)

An almost alarmingly open and honest song, this early glimpse into the world of Brian Wilson boasts group vocals which poignantly underline his resigned self-assessment of his hopes and fears. Maureen Love again supplies harp, and as the B-side to 'Be True To Your School', this Four Freshmen-styled ballad was a Top 30 hit in its own right, and remains a concert staple. The 5th CD of the 1993 box set opens with a studio demo of this track, a somewhat different arrangement.

HAWAII
(B.Wilson/Love*)

Another Brian Wilson/Mike Love vocal duet, more frenetic than intellectual.

SURFER'S RULE
(B.Wilson/Love)

Ostensibly a surfers/greasers rivalry tune, with the only true surfer in the band, Dennis Wilson, fittingly taking the lead vocal. The authentic-sounding Four Seasons pastiche at the end of each verse suggests that Brian Wilson was beginning to harbour a rivalry of trans-continental proportions. A truce would be called in 1983 when The Beach Boys and The Four Seasons combined on a truly superb one-off single, 'East Meets West'.

OUR CAR CLUB
(B.Wilson/Love)

With a drum track beyond Dennis Wilson's capability and a sax arrangement equally too complex for Love, it's safe to assume that Hal Blaine and Steve Douglas feature here. In fact, the whole arrangement exhibits remarkable musical – and vocal – progression from the band that had recorded 'Surfin'' less than two years previously. Brian Wilson and Love again share vocal chores on a song originally logged as 'Rabbit's Foot'; Brian's habit of titling instrumental tracks with the first idea that came into his head has caused confusion and heartache to generations of Beach Boys historians.

YOUR SUMMER DREAM
(B.Wilson/Norberg)

Completely different from the preceding track, yet equally innovative, this gentle ballad featured the vocal talents of Brian Wilson alone.

BOOGIE WOODIE
(Rimsky-Korsakov, arr. B.Wilson)

Somewhere in here is 'The Flight Of The Bumble Bee', reworked in a style still beloved of Brian Wilson to this day. Filler? Perhaps, but amusing nonetheless.

IN MY ROOM+ (GERMAN LANGUAGE VERSION)
(B.Wilson/Usher)

The Beach Boys were long rumoured to have recorded in German, just as The Beatles did, but proof wasn't forthcoming until the release in 1983 of this track on the 'Rarities' album (see below). Even auf Deutsch, the beauty of the song – and performance – shines through.

LITTLE DEUCE COUPE
(CAPITOL ST-1998 [LP] CDP 7 93693 2 [CD];
RELEASED OCTOBER 1963)

"Whenever there's a new fad, we'll be riding it," Brian Wilson observed in the early Sixties, perhaps to explain why, only a month after 'Surfer Girl', The Beach Boys released a new(-ish) album celebrating not waves and babes but rather cars (and babes), and arguably the world's first ever concept album, given that all the tracks (with one excusable exception), concerned cars and the potential thereof. Repeating two cuts from an LP released little more than thirty days previously (plus one track apiece from each of their first two LPs) could be seen as either slacking off or gypping the punters, were it not for the fact that the new songs (all recorded in one day, according to the session information) are adequate at worst, and sometimes excellent, continuing the improvement evident on 'Surfer Girl'.

The change of theme was also a shrewd move on Brian's part – while most of America could only dream about riding the waves, cruising the local drag was a national teen pre-occupation, and the album struck an instant chord countrywide, going Top 5 in the US and selling over a million copies during a chart life of almost a year, but missing the UK chart. Although David Marks obviously appears on the four previously released tracks, the new material marks the official return to the band of Alan Jardine.

LITTLE DEUCE COUPE
(B.Wilson/Christian)

See 'Surfer Girl' album.

BALLAD OF OLE' BETSY
(B.Wilson/Christian)

Brian waxing so maudlin over a mere pile of metal and rubber might seem preposterous, were it not for the fact that some *did* lavish such affection on their rods… and for the sumptuous vocals throughout the song.

BE TRUE TO YOUR SCHOOL
(B.Wilson/Love*)

The only track on the album not explicitly mentioning cars (although "cruisin'" is mentioned) elevates loyalty to a near-evangelical level and over thirty years later, remains a concert favourite. The almost martial intro and cheer-leading backing vocals underpinning one of Love's best lead vocals to date create an early-period classic. The 5th CD of the boxed set includes a rather shaky live version from 1964 (performed as per the single version (see below)).

CAR CRAZY CUTIE
(B.Wilson/Christian)

Originally cut by Brian Wilson, Bob Norberg and others as the much more energetic 'Pamela Jean' – released in January, 1964, as The Survivors – this Dion-esque number was hijacked by its creator when 'Little Deuce Coupe' needed extra songs. Strangely, the version here, while energetic, doesn't measure up to the original, despite great group vocals, and Wilson's own neat lead.

CHERRY, CHERRY COUPE
(B.Wilson/Christian)

Another retread, of the then-unreleased "Land Ahoy", this is a superior second try. Love handles some seriously technical lyrics with considerable aplomb.

409
(B.Wilson/Usher/Love*)

See 'Surfin' Safari' album.

SHUT DOWN
(B.Wilson/Christian)

See 'Surfin' USA' album.

SPIRIT OF AMERICA
(B.Wilson/Christian)

In the early Sixties, the Americans attempting to capture the World Land Speed Record upped the stakes by using jet-powered cars rather than piston engined machines, with the results described by Brian Wilson here in Roger Christian's journalistic lyric.

OUR CAR CLUB
(B.Wilson/Love)

See 'Surfer Girl' album.

NO-GO SHOWBOAT
(B.Wilson/Christian)

Possibly the best cut on the album, with sterling vocals from Brian Wilson and Love, lyrics neatly combining jargon with humour, and a snorting melody. Musically rather more complex than may at first appear.

A YOUNG MAN IS GONE
(Troup/Love)

The original Capitol demo tape included a version of Bobby Troup's 'Their Hearts Were Full Of Spring' (finally released on the 1993 boxed set) – which the band would later perform flawlessly in concert – but for this tribute to James Dean, Love wrote new lyrics, and the group supplied their first, and possibly best, a cappella outing. Stunning.

CUSTOM MACHINE
(B.Wilson)

Reportedly these detailed lyrics were supplied by Rich Alarian (of The Survivors). Love and the group pitch in with the now customary verve and expertise.

BE TRUE TO YOUR SCHOOL+ (45 VERSION)
(B.Wilson/Love*)

This completely re-recorded version (not an alternate mix, as is sometimes stated) was a late 1963 US Top 10 hit. Rearranged to sound even more like a marching band, and featuring not only The Honeys (the female trio which included the future Mrs. Brian Wilson) as cheerleaders but also a snatch of the Hawthorne High football fight song during the bridge, this is possibly one of Love's best uptempo leads, and definitely one of its writer's more inspired retreads.

mono

Capitol Records HIGH FIDELITY

FUN, FUN, FUN
IN THE PARKIN' LOT
POM, POM PLAY GIRL ★ THIS CAR
OF MINE ★ SHUT DOWN, PART II
"CASSIUS" LOVE VS "SONNY" WILSON

SHUT DOWN
VOLUME 2

the beach boys

WHY DO FOOLS FALL IN LOVE
THE WARMTH OF THE SUN
DON'T WORRY BABY
DENNY'S DRUMS ★ LOUIE, LOUIE
KEEP AN EYE ON SUMMER

SHUT DOWN VOLUME 2

(CAPITOL ST-2027 [LP] CDP 7 93692 2 [CD]; RELEASED MARCH 1964)

Even when the hits were flowing, The Beach Boys and Capitol Records never enjoyed the best of relationships, and the label's decision to issue – without the band's knowledge – an album called 'Shut Down' in the summer of 1963 utilising just two Beach Boys cuts ('409' and the title track) alongside car songs by the likes of Robert Mitchum (correct, the actor) and those well known LA bands, The Cheers and The Super Stocks, as well as The Piltdown Men (a group of studio musicians reputed to work mainly on Frank Sinatra sessions) hardly helped matters. It was reasonably successful, reaching the US Top 10 (possibly because many purchasers thought it was a new Beach Boys album...) and could have been the spur for 'Little Deuce Coupe' to be constructed at such high speed. To underline their point, the band decided to title their first album of 1964 'Shut Down Volume 2'.

Despite including some of Brian Wilson's most gorgeous ballads to date, plus one of their most instantly recognisable numbers, the album has a rushed, half-hearted feel to it, especially towards the end, something the US chart placing (Top 20, after three consecutive Top 10 LPs in the previous six months) reflected. It also missed the UK chart.

FUN, FUN, FUN
(B.Wilson/Love)

From the ringing intro (played by Glen Campbell) to the wailing fadeout, this may just be the ultimate cruisin' singalong and accordingly went Top 5 in America (only their second single to get that high). Everything fits, from Love's cocky vocal through the powerful harmonies to the driving backing track. Reputedly written specifically as a reply to the then rampant Beatlemania, the lyrics supposedly tell a true story about a girl-friend of Dennis Wilson. A 24-carat classic, then and forever.

DON'T WORRY, BABY
(B.Wilson/Christian)

Allegedly written for The Ronettes (but declined by Phil Spector), this sumptuous US Top 30 ballad (B side of 'I Get Around') is the peak of Brian Wilson's work with Roger Christian, and not at all coincidentally may be viewed as the start of a move away from such narrow themes as cars. Thrilling harmonies, with Brian's lead icing the cake. This was surf fanatic Keith Moon's all time favourite song and The Who's demon drummer covered it with distressing results on his only solo album in 1975.

IN THE PARKIN' LOT
(B.Wilson/Christian)

Bookended by stunning harmonies, this fre-netic track tries really hard and has some nice moments but never really convinces. There's a rushed air about it, most notably in Love's

lead vocal... but following 'Don't Worry Baby', almost anything would be an anti-climax.

"CASSIUS" LOVE VS. "SONNY" WILSON
(Love/B.Wilson)

Amusing once or twice, this painfully contrived piece of "audio-verité" swiftly palls. The title refers to the world heavyweight championship fight between Cassius Clay (later known as Muhammad Ali) and Sonny Liston, who was expected to retain his crown. Clay won the real fight, but the result of the imaginary musi-cal bout was less clearcut. The studio feuding between Love and Brian Wilson would soon be for real...

THE WARMTH OF THE SUN
(B.Wilson/Love)

Composed a few hours after the assassina-tion of President John F.Kennedy in November, 1963, Brian Wilson's yearning vocal and the lush harmony cushion arguably express perfectly a sense of overwhelming loss. A hidden gem.

THIS CAR OF MINE
(B.Wilson/Love)

Strong vocals from Dennis Wilson and excellent block harmonies cannot rescue a song which sounds incomplete and uninspired.

WHY DO FOOLS FALL IN LOVE?
(Lymon)

A doo-wop classic and a giant international hit for Frankie Lymon and The Teenagers in 1956, one of the better Beach Boys cover versions, a soaring falsetto lead from Brian Wilson, and, unaccountably, a mono track on a stereo album.

POM POM PLAYGIRL
(B.Wilson/Love)

It's a shame The Beach Boys never attempted a 'high school' album along the lines of 'Little Deuce Coupe', as Love definitely had a lyrical feel for the genre. A somewhat lower key vocal from Brian Wilson than usual.

KEEP AN EYE ON SUMMER
(B.Wilson/Norberg/Love)

Inspiration begins to wane; it's very easy on the ear, and Brian Wilson's lead is as sweet as ever, but it's déjà-vu time, and this is aimlessly inoffensive. Bob Norberg's co-credit hints at the age of the song.

SHUT DOWN PART II
(C.Wilson)

The return of the instrumental. Love reprises his two-note sax solo, Carl Wilson weighs in with some decent licks, but that's about it – filler.

LOUIE, LOUIE
(Berry)

A listless cover of The Kingsmen's garage classic (the Berry is Richard, not Chuck) with Love in decidedly average vocal form.

DENNY'S DRUMS
(D.Wilson)

Possibly the first drum solo ever recorded in the rock field... but is it Dennis Wilson? Another mono track.

FUN, FUN, FUN+
(45 MONO MIX)
(B.Wilson/Love)

As approved (and improved) by Brian Wilson, with impressive falsetto wails over the extended fade.

I DO+
(B.Wilson)

Later recorded and released by the Castells – produced by Brian Wilson – this was apparently going to be a Beach Boys track. All the singing, Brian Wilson and Mike Love's leads included, sound like guide vocals. The Castells' version used this backing track.

ALL SUMMER LONG
(CAPITOL ST-2110 [LP] CDP 7 93693 2 [CD];
RELEASED JULY 1964)

As if to atone for the relative commercial and creative disappointment of 'Shut Down, Volume 2', The Beach Boys bounced straight back with their most satisfying album to date and the second to display a coherent theme... but where 'Little Deuce Coupe' celebrated the narrow automotive world, 'All Summer Long' encapsulated almost perfectly the Southern Californian experience, additionally showcasing some startling musical advances. Brian Wilson's apparently necessary breathing space was over, and his compositions began to take wing in the most unexpected – and exhilarating – manner and direction. As a farewell to cars and surfin', it's impeccable... as a portent of glories to come, it's tantalising. As merely a damn good mid-Sixties album, it's simply among the best by anyone, and was the group's third US Top 5 LP (out of six thus far), remaining in the charts for nearly a year, but still a UK flop.

I GET AROUND
(B.Wilson/Love)

The band's first US chart-topper (and first UK Top 10 hit), and a major milestone in Brian Wilson's evolving writing and production style, 'I Get Around' is simultaneously vintage Beach Boys and unlike anything they'd done before. Beneath the deceptively simplistic lyric lies a highly sophisticated backing track of great complexity; coupled with a spirited lead from Love and almost percussive harmonies, the overall effect is awesome. No true stereo mix is known to exist; however, the instrumental track alone was included in the 'Good Vibrations' 5 CD boxed set... but it's actually the track the band had to recut for the 'Concert!' album, and not the original!

ALL SUMMER LONG
(B.Wilson/Love*)

Cheerfully sloppy vocally – almost to the point of dissonance – and lyrically engaging, this rattles along propelled by xylophone, piccolo and Love's exuberant lead. Once again, a true stereo mix has yet to surface, but one is possible, as the release of the boxed set proves: included were five songs remixed into a "backing-on-the-left/vocals-on-the-right" format (hereafter referred to as 'vocal splits'), of which this is one.

HUSHABYE
(Pomus/Shuman)

Brian Wilson reached new heights of vocal arranging on this glorious cover of the 1959 US Top 20 hit by The Mystics, and the rest of the band were in superlative vocal form. Although Love and Wilson are credited as lead vocalists, everybody should take a bow. Two new versions of 'Hushabye' surfaced on the 1993 boxed set, a live recording from 1964 and a stunning vocal split mix.

LITTLE HONDA
(B.Wilson/Love)

A pioneering use of fuzz-tone, an urgent lead from Love and forceful backing vocals accelerate this song, at one time intended as a single, which eventually appeared on the band's only official US EP, and was a minor hit.

WE'LL RUN AWAY
(B.Wilson/Usher)

Probably dating from two years earlier, this ballad features an unusual Hammond organ sound underscoring an expertly double-tracked Brian Wilson lead vocal.

CARL'S BIG CHANCE
(B.Wilson/C.Wilson)

The band's final surf-styled instrumental, notable for the droning sax and seemingly improvised guitar lines from Carl, the youngest Wilson brother.

WENDY
(B.Wilson/Love*)

An ominous three-note phrase precedes classic group harmonies and a less than cheerful lyric handled by Love and Brian Wilson, overlaying unusual chord changes. This stereo mix features the famous "middle-eight cough" absent from the mono version. Like 'Little Honda', this was included on '4 By The Beach Boys', a US Top 50 EP. A vocal split version, with the cough intact, appeared on the boxed set.

DO YOU REMEMBER?
(B.Wilson/Love*)

A mildly revisionist recounting of rock'n'roll history – and, incidentally, of the band's own influences – with Love and Brian Wilson in sparkling vocal form. No great art here, just plain good fun.

GIRLS ON THE BEACH
(B.Wilson)

A powerful slow ballad and the title song of a movie featuring The Beach Boys, this is 'Warmth Of The Sun' with a positive outlook, the group vocal highlighted by Dennis Wilson's earnest middle eight.

DRIVE-IN
(B.Wilson/Love*)

Huge fun in all respects, yet boasting unexpected dead air after the instrumental break, this reportedly remains one of Brian Wilson's favourite songs. Love handles the double tracking expertly... and for those who may be wondering, "only *you* can prevent forest fires" comes from a 'Barney The Bear' fire prevention cartoon.

OUR FAVOURITE RECORDING SESSIONS
(B.Wilson/C.Wilson/
D.Wilson/Jardine/Love)

Another peek inside the studio as our Boys set to work, less forced than the previous 'Cassius' Love *vs.* 'Sonny' Wilson, but still best sampled infrequently. 'Charlie' is Western Studios engineer Charles M. (Chuck) Britz.

DON'T BACK DOWN
(B.Wilson/Love*)

The Beach Boys last surf-themed song for four years closes the era with considerable panache. Brian Wilson's chorus could be self-admonishing ("show 'em now who's got guts") while Love handles the verses with ease. Twilight zone time – on the first pressing of the LP, the title on the front of the sleeve was 'Don't Break Down'; five months later, Brian Wilson did just that.

ALL DRESSED UP FOR SCHOOL+
(B.Wilson)

Shelved in 1964, perhaps due to its slightly non-PC lyric, lead vocalist Brian Wilson later recycled parts of the melody in such songs as 'Heroes And Villains', 'Goin' On', 'I Just Got My Pay', 'Marcella' and a Honda 55 commercial (apparently never used). Somewhat atypical of Beach Boys vintage 1964.

LITTLE HONDA+
ALTERNATIVE VERSION
(B.Wilson/Love*)

This variation features more involved, and possibly better, backing vocals.

DON'T BACK DOWN+
(ALTERNATE VERSION)
(B.Wilson/Love*)

"Different song" would be a better description: melody, lyrics and vocals are utterly unlike the released track, leading one to believe that – if the session information is accurate – Brian Wilson and the band totally revamped the song in the studio.

THE BEACH BOYS'
CHRISTMAS ALBUM
(CAPITOL ST 2164 [LP] CDP 7 91008 2 [CD];
RELEASED OCTOBER 1964)

The success of 1963's seasonal single, 'Little Saint Nick', a Top 3 hit in the special Xmas Billboard chart, made a full blown Christmas album inevitable, especially from a band once labelled "rock's only true choir". Brian Wilson's decision to mix standards and new material might have been a canny ploy to cover all the bases, or an early step into the mainstream. Whatever, the result was – the restrictions of the genre allowing – more than adequate on all counts. For many years, the understanding was that Brian had arranged the 40-piece orchestra featured on the standards, a strange myth, as the name of arranger Dick Reynolds is writ large on the original LP sleeve! The album briefly reached the seasonal US chart each Christmas between 1964 and 1968, its highest position coming in 1964 when it went Top 10. This CD reissue, while excellent in all other respects, goes slightly pear-shaped over the matter of mono vs. stereo. Basically, everything except 'Little Saint Nick (LP mix)' of the Wilson originals is mono, though listed as stereo.

LITTLE SAINT NICK
(B.Wilson/Love*)

A bona-fide Christmas perennial, defying time and fashion, propelled by the now-familiar 'Little Deuce Coupe' backbeat. A perky lead from Love... however, this isn't the single mix.

THE MAN WITH ALL THE TOYS
(B.Wilson/Love*)

A glorious a cappella break can't really lift this well-intentioned item above the mundane level. Love and Brian Wilson trade off the lead vocal.

SANTA'S BEARD
(B.Wilson/Love*)

Wonderful harmonies and some neat counter-vocals restore the festive mood on this sad tale of childhood betrayed. Love again has trouble with the double tracking on yet another variation on the 1-2-3-4 theme.

MERRY CHRISTMAS, BABY
(B.Wilson/Love*)

A strangely uptempo tale of love lost – with an equally inconsequential chorus – on which Love takes the lead vocal.

CHRISTMAS DAY
(B.Wilson)

Alan Jardine's début lead vocal on a Beach Boys song matches the material – neither are exactly top notch.

FROSTY THE SNOWMAN
(Nelson/Rollins)

The first of the orchestral tracks finds the group in sparkling vocal form. The arrangement is decidedly Forties, and none the worse for that. Joyous.

WE THREE KINGS OF ORIENT ARE
(Hopkins)

Easily the outstanding track on the album, an atmospheric arrangement is matched by sumptuous moving harmony blocks. Spine-chillingly magnificent in every respect, especially the a cappella tag.

BLUE CHRISTMAS
(Hayes/Johnson)

Maybe the arrangement is a mite too upbeat, maybe Brian Wilson's lead is a touch too pristine, but if somehow this fails to totally convince, it's never less than pleasant.

SANTA CLAUS IS COMING TO TOWN
(Coots/Gillespie)

Back to the 1940s, with an arrangement sadly betrayed by Love's carelessly nasal lead; maybe he had a cold that day... The rest of the band chip in to great effect.

WHITE CHRISTMAS
(Berlin)

Inevitable. Of course, there can only be one version of this, but Brian Wilson still turns in a perfectly fine performance.

I'LL BE HOME FOR CHRISTMAS
(Kent/Gannon)

A strangely mournful rendering, yet one that somehow seems to suit the band's voices. A thoughtful reading.

AULD LANG SYNE
(Traditional)

As much as everyone loved Dennis Wilson, his seasonal greetings slightly mar a marvellous piece of group harmony... but hell, it's Christmas – he's forgiven.

LITTLE SAINT NICK+45 MIX
(B.Wilson/Love*)

A mono reprise of the opening track, replete with glockenspiel and sleighbell overdubs strangely absent from the album version.

THE LORD'S PRAYER+
(Malotte)

A first appearance in stereo for the B-side of the 'Little Saint Nick' 45. Beautiful in its complexity.

LITTLE SAINT NICK+
(ALTERNATE TAKE)
(B.Wilson/Love*)

This time, the melody is that of 'Drive-In' (from the 'All Summer Long' LP), prompting the question "which came first?" Answer – no-one knows. Obviously a less than serious attempt.

AULD LANG SYNE+ (ALTER-NATE TAKE)
(Traditional)

Dennis Wilson excised! Taken from a Capitol sampler – hence the grainy mono sound quality – and the band shine when laid bare.

THE BEACH BOYS' CONCERT
(CAPITOL STAO 2198 [LP] CDP 7 935695 2 [CD]; RELEASED OCTOBER 1964)

The first Beach Boys album to top the US chart was recorded in Sacramento, a Northern California hotbed of Beach Boys fever some 95 miles inland, and proves conclusively, from first note to last, that they were a great live band. Carl Wilson's guitar licks, Brian Wilson's soaring falsetto, and even Dennis Wilson's drumming are well up to scratch... not that too much could be heard over the screaming! And, unlike some albums, this response isn't an engineering wheeze – in fact, the crowd noise was actually mixed down, and even so, a couple of tracks had to be 'doctored' in the studio ('I Get Around' most obviously) to rise above the screams. The introduction is by Fred Vail, who later became a vital part of the band's touring set-up, and an especially close friend of Dennis.

FUN, FUN, FUN
(B.Wilson/Love)

See 'Shut Down, Volume 2' album.

THE LITTLE OLD LADY FROM PASADENA
(Atfield/Christian)

One of the few Sixties hits for Jan & Dean that Brian Wilson didn't have a hand in writing, this item has returned to the band's live set in the 1990s as part of the car medley. Love sang it rather better then.

LITTLE DEUCE COUPE
(B.Wilson/Christian)

See 'Surfer Girl' album.

LONG TALL TEXAN
(Strzlecki)

A small US success for little known one-hit-wonder Murry Kellum in 1963, this close relation to 'Hi-Heel Sneakers' has aged with very little grace; ditto Love's lead... but the crowd loved it. So that's OK then...

IN MY ROOM
(B.Wilson/Usher)

See 'Surfer Girl' album.

MONSTER MASH
(Pickett/Capizzi)

A novelty US #1 from 1962 by Bobby 'Boris' Pickett given the Hawthorne once-over. Dennis Wilson's style is just perfect here, as is Love's best Vincent Price impression. Great fun.

LET'S GO TRIPPIN'
(Dale)

See 'Surfin' USA' album.

PAPA-OOM-MOW-MOW
(Frazier/White/Wilson/Harris)

Both Love and Brian Wilson attempt to seriously damage their vocal chords on this raucous cover of the 1962 garage band classic by Los Angeles quartet The Rivingtons.

THE WANDERER
(Maresca)

A then recent US Top 5 hit for Dion, taken at a rapid clip by vocalist Dennis Wilson. A not inappropriate choice, in view of Dennis's restless heart.

HAWAII
(B.Wilson/Love*)

See 'Surfer Girl' album.

GRADUATION DAY
(Sherman/Sherman)

Brian Wilson's tip of the hat towards The Four Freshmen, one of his main influences, is as expert as it is reverential. The off-key interjection at the end is – of course – Dennis Wilson.

I GET AROUND
(B.Wilson/Love*)

See 'All Summer Long' album.

JOHNNY B.GOODE
(Berry)

Does the intro sound familiar? A rattling cover of the Chuck Berry classic finds Carl Wilson in cracking form on the guitar

DON'T WORRY, BABY+
(B.Wilson/Christian)

Perhaps not the best live version of this lovely song you'll ever hear, but probably the only one with Brian Wilson in good voice.

HEROES AND VILLAINS+
(B.Wilson/Parks)

Strictly speaking out of sequence, this 1967 Hawaii performance of a song released little over a month previously features the five original group members (Bruce Johnston stayed home) making a very fair fist of presenting their most complex number to date live in concert... and Brian Wilson's obvious enjoyment is something of a revelation. Not as involved as later live versions, perhaps.

THE BEACH BOYS TODAY!

PLEASE LET ME WONDER · GOOD TO MY BABY · DANCE, DANCE, DANCE · WHEN I GROW UP
SHE KNOWS ME TOO WELL · HELP ME, RONDA · KISS ME, BABY · DO YOU WANNA DANCE?
DON'T HURT MY LITTLE SISTER...plus three more great new songs written by Brian Wilson

THE BEACH BOYS TODAY!

(CAPITOL T 2269 [LP] CDP 93694 2 [CD]; RELEASED MARCH 1965)

Peaking in the US Top 5/UK Top 10, this impressive album became the group's sixth US Top 10 LP in under two years, but it was significant for other reasons. December 23, 1964, is a key date in Beach Boys history, as Brian Wilson, married only 16 days, suffered his first breakdown on a flight to Houston, Texas. On returning home, he decided that the only way that he – and the band – could progress creatively was for him to retire from touring to concentrate on composing and producing while the others continued on the road. His initial replacement, until April, 1965, was guitarist Glen Campbell, a veteran of many Beach Boys sessions.

'Today!' is generally referred to as Brian's first post-touring album, a claim not entirely accurate as four of the songs had been recorded prior to the Houston episode. More pertinent was the proclamation on the LP's back cover – "A program of big Beach Boy favourites... plus some great new Brian Wilson songs". To further underscore the point, the original vinyl issue gathered the uptempo numbers on one side, the ballads on the other, resulting in the band's best offering to date, with only one "filler" track. The uptempo songs were everything fans had come to expect from The Beach Boys, but it was in the ballads that Brian's – and the band's – future direction lay. The path to 'Pet Sounds' was clearly signposted...

No true stereo version of 'The Beach Boys Today!' has ever been issued, nor is one known to exist.

DO YOU WANNA DANCE?
(Freeman)

A US Top 20 single in early 1965, Dennis Wilson's handling of Bobby Freeman's 1958 hit is note-perfect, as is his double-tracking.

Astonishing as it may seem, collectors' tapes reveal that lead and backing vocals for this song were recorded simultaneously.

GOOD TO MY BABY
(B.Wilson/Love*)

A terrific bass vocal intro from Love sets the tone for this cheery rocker. The instrumental track is deceptively simple, leaving ample room for swooping harmonies. Brian Wilson's lead vocal is pretty neat, too.

DON'T HURT MY LITTLE SISTER
(B.Wilson/Love*)

Rebuffed with 'Don't Worry, Baby', Brian Wilson wrote another song for Spector's Ronettes, only to have Phil rework it into 'Things Are Changing (For The Better)', eventually released by The Blossoms. Allegedly based on a remark his sister-in-law made to Brian, this would have been outstanding on any previous Beach Boys album... here, it's merely good.

WHEN I GROW UP (TO BE A MAN)
(B.Wilson/Love*)

The unusual subject matter – ageing – may have evolved from a recording that was astonishingly advanced for the time, driven by a harpsichord and underpinned by a drum pattern of unorthodox complexity... and the vocal arrangement matches, especially on the chorus. Elsewhere on the verse, Love does a sterling job. A US Top 10/UK Top 30 single, it was the group's sixth to reach the US Top 10. A vocal split version, released on the 1993 boxed set, allows the instrumental track to be heard in all its magnificence.

HELP ME, RONDA
(B.Wilson/Love*)

Regarded as Alan Jardine's first "proper" lead vocal, 'Ronda' (sic) is one of the band's most popular hits, still guaranteeing an instant audience response well into the Nineties. This is the original album (i.e. non-hit) version, but it's still great fun, especially the harmonica riff.

DANCE, DANCE, DANCE
(B.Wilson/C.Wilson/ Love*)

A US Top 10 single in late 1964 (UK Top 30 in January, 1965), the opening bass riff launches into the musical cousin of 'Do You Wanna Dance?' Another driving item crowned by great group harmonies and a classic Love lead vocal: the unadorned instrumental track appeared on the boxed set.

PLEASE LET ME WONDER
(B.Wilson/Love)

Opening the original "ballad side" of 'Today!' is another naïve sentiment from Brian Wilson, whose lead vocal may be one of the sweetest he's ever recorded. Angelic backing vocals complete the mood.

I'M SO YOUNG
(Tyrus)

Brian Wilson's take on an original 1950s song by The Students enables it to sit comfortably among his own ballads, due mainly to the lush harmonies.

KISS ME, BABY
(B.Wilson/Love*)

The hidden highlight of 'Today!', with the two songwriters trading lead vocals to exquisite effect over an inventively percussive backing that wouldn't sound out of place on 'Pet Sounds'. Nor would the lyrics, come to that, a perfect example of teen angst. Brian Wilson reportedly composed the basic melody on the piano in an Amsterdam brothel during the band's 1964 European visit (it should be pointed out that, struck by the muse whilst out strolling, he dashed into the nearest place with a piano, which just happened to be a cathouse, of which there are many in central Amsterdam).

SHE KNOWS ME TOO WELL
(B.Wilson/Love*)

A companion to the preceding track in both subject and treatment, and another milestone on the 'Pet Sounds' road, this gorgeous ballad has a strangely questioning air about it. Brian Wilson's vocal is sweetly resigned.

IN THE BACK OF MY MIND
(B.Wilson/Love*)

Behind Dennis Wilson's plaintive vocal – a perfect use of his expressive tones – is a stunningly complex instrumental track deserving of better exposure. Even though the tag appears to belong to another song, it still fits. Superb in all departments.

BULL SESSION WITH "BIG DADDY"
(B.Wilson/C.Wilson/
D.Wilson/Love/Jardine)

The third, and thankfully last, of the talk tracks forms a bizarre coda to the ballad sequence. The 'Big Daddy' is Earl Leaf, a journalist and absolutely no relation to Brian Wilson's biographer, David Leaf.

DANCE, DANCE, DANCE+ (ALTERNATE TAKE)
(B.Wilson/C.Wilson/
Love*)

Recorded in Nashville a month before the 'real' version, this features the band playing the instrumental track... and the difference really isn't that great. The lyric is slightly altered, and this version is in stereo.

I'M SO YOUNG+ (ALTERNATE TAKE)
(Tyrus)

Also in stereo, this early version features a flute riff, a more prominent bass and truly dodgy drumming.

SUMMER DAYS (AND SUMMER NIGHTS !!)

(CAPITOL T 235 [LP] CDP 7 93694 2 [CD];
RELEASED JUNE 1965)

After touring with The Beach Boys for three months, and despite being offered a permanent place in the touring band, Glen Campbell decided to return to session work. His replacement was Bruce Johnston, a long-standing member of the Los Angeles music scene with a recording history actually predating that of The Beach Boys. Compatible with the band musically and personally, Johnston settled in immediately and the sessions for this album were his first studio work as a Beach Boy.

Coming hard on the heels of 'Today!' – especially the ballads – 'Summer Days' is often viewed as something of a sideways step in the musical evolution of Brian Wilson, and certainly the second side of the original LP seemed less inspired. However, the key word is "seemed", for in mid-1965, Wilson was in a mood of such artistic power that even material he considered throwaway was, for the aver-age songwriter, almost worth dying for. Whether or not he consciously bowed one last time to Capitol's urgings for more commercial gold, or was simply leaning back and taking it easy, matters not; even at half-throttle, Brian Wilson in mid-1965 was an awesome force.

Released less than four months after 'Today!' (and the group would release a third 1965 LP another four months later!), 'Summer Days' became the band's eighth gold LP in well under two and a half years, remaining in the US Top 200 for around eight months and becoming their fourth LP to reach the Top 5 in twelve months. It is worth noting that by this time, The Beatles had conquered the United States, and at the time of the release of 'Summer Days', had released 14 US chart LPs (some non-musical) in under 18 months. For The Beach Boys to merely survive amid the so-called "British Invasion" of beat groups was a considerable achievement, and to actively prosper in those circumstances was exceptional. In Britain, this LP was not released until after 'Pet Sounds', becoming their third UK Top 5 LP of 1966.

THE GIRL FROM NEW YORK CITY
(B.Wilson/Love*)

Energetic – that's the word. Love's lead, the chorus harmonies, Brian Wilson's soaring falsetto and a forcefully sparse track combine to supply a cracking opening to any album. The sax probably isn't played by Love, and the subject of the song is generally reckoned to be Lesley Gore, who was indeed born in New York City, and had turned many heads in 1963 with her US chart-topping 45, 'It's My Party'.

AMUSEMENT PARKS USA
(B.Wilson/Love*)

'County Fair' three years on... and the improvement is astounding. Mob-handed group vocals hook the listener and Love keeps a firm grip, aided by Brian Wilson (who also provides the hysterical laughter). As per 'Surfin' USA', the Boys name-check the nation's most popular funfairs over a melody similar to 'Palisades Park', the 1962 Freddy Cannon hit. Wonderful stuff. According to Brian, the carnival "barker" is legendary session drummer Hal Blaine.

THEN I KISSED HER
(Spector/Greenwich/ Barry)

A surprisingly restrained and faithful cover of The Crystals US Top 10 classic, 'Then He Kissed Me', finds Alan Jardine (probably the lowest profile band member prior to Bruce Johnston joining) in fine vocal form. Released as a single in the UK only to plug the nine months gap between 'Good Vibrations' and 'Heroes And Villains', it reached the Top 5, the group's fifth consecutive 45 to peak so high in under 18 months. Heavy on the echo pot.

SALT LAKE CITY
(B.Wilson/Love*)

For some unaccountable reason, The Beach Boys have always seemed to be more popular inland, where the surf is never up. Lyrically obvious (to the point where Salt Lake City's Downtown Merchant's Association used the song as a promotional item), there's a lot going on underneath the vocals (by Love and Brian Wilson) deserving wider exposure. Nifty harmonies.

GIRL, DON'T TELL ME
(B.Wilson)

Astonishingly, this was Carl Wilson's first lead vocal on a studio album! Heavily influenced by The Beatles, and none the worse for that, this song is something of an oddity for the period in that The Beach Boys actually play, as well as sing on it. An alternate, less Beatlesque, version remains unreleased.

HELP ME, RHONDA
(B.Wilson/Love*)

Not only the spelling of R(h)onda differs on the group's second US Number One single (merely Top 30 in Britain), this is a reworking of a song from the previous 'Today!' LP: revised backing vocals, a chiming guitar riff and the omission of the harmonica help to make this a definitive Brian Wilson production.

CALIFORNIA GIRLS
(B.Wilson/Love*)

From the stately, quasi-symphonic opening riff to the closing vocal cascade, 'California Girls' has become The Beach Boys' theme tune,

even more than 'Good Vibrations'. It's irresistible, never breaking out of a brisk stroll, but with vocals and harmonies (with new boy Bruce Johnston clearly audible) so forceful as to be pushy... and the backing track is no slouch either, as 'Stack-O-Tracks' confirms. To watch the band play this song live in California, and observe the sheer euphoria of the girls in the audience, is to approach Beach Boys nirvana. The girls don't just sing the words, they sing the guitar parts too!

Initially titled 'I Love The Girls', one session tape has Brian Wilson bizarrely calling it 'You Are My Lawn And I Am The Mower', whilst another names it 'We Don't Know'! Researchers beware. Highlights of the "collectors" CD in the boxed set were the unmixed vocal tracks in glorious stereo. Released as a single, it was a US Top 5/UK Top 30 hit: The Beach Boys were comparative novices in UK chart terms before 1966.

LET HIM RUN WILD
(B.Wilson/Love*)

The previous title notwithstanding, this is the album's highlight, and another step towards

'Pet Sounds'. A complex yet never obscure backing track underpins an off-beat vocal arrangement, and each stunningly counterpoints the other. Brian Wilson's lead vocal, pitched just this side of shrill, tops a sublime, yet lyrically strong, confection.

YOU'RE SO GOOD TO ME
(B.Wilson/Love*)

Suffering in comparison with the preceding gem, this straightforward rocker – unusually simple for the period – featuring Brian Wilson's strong lead vocal would have seemed more than adequate on almost anyone else's LP of the time. Its inclusion on 'Best Of The Beach Boys', the group's first big selling UK compilation LP, always seemed odd (says JT).

SUMMER MEANS NEW LOVE
(B.Wilson)

With this instrumental, Brian Wilson was evidently extending his musical scope beyond basic rock'n'roll. A slightly awkward air prevails, suggesting either a rushed session or an evolutionary track. Nonetheless, charming, if gauche.

I'M BUGGED AT MY OL' MAN
(B.Wilson)

With only an accompanying piano and decidedly unpolished assistance from the rest of the band, Brian Wilson outlines a series of extraordinary complaints against his father, Murry. Sadly, there was more than a grain of truth in the lyric.

AND YOUR DREAM COMES TRUE
(B.Wilson/Love)

Based on the nursery rhyme 'Baa Baa Black Sheep', the band are in superb form on this gorgeous a cappella piece. Magical – at least three bags full.

THE LITTLE GIRL I ONCE KNEW+
(B.Wilson)

'Let Him Run Wild' taken several steps further results in another subtly complex number of great beauty, with the dead air of 'Drive-In', a cyclical organ pattern, a knockout bass from Love and crystalline vocals from the rest of the band, while the intro alone assumes clas sic status. Perhaps because of the dead air, released as a single it only just made the US Top 20 and totally stiffed in Britain.

LET HIM RUN WILD+
(ALTERNATE TAKE)
(B.Wilson/Love*)

The backing vocals are the only real difference here... and it's still a stunning track.

GRADUATION DAY+
(STUDIO VERSION)
(Sherman/Sherman)

Recorded at the same session as 'Amusement Parks USA', this truly reverential pass at The Four Freshmen vocal harmony classic utilises minimal accompaniment and maximum vocal expertise, and is the only track on the CD in stereo.

BEACH BOYS PARTY!
(CAPITOL DMAS 2398 [LP] CDP 7 93698 2 [CD]; RELEASED NOVEMBER 1965)

Brian Wilson was in pre-production for 'Pet Sounds' when Capitol made it abundantly clear that a new Beach Boys album was required before Xmas – or else! Wilson had neither the material nor the inclination to knuckle down just yet, and a standoff seemed inevitable... until some unsung hero provided an acceptable compromise: a "live-in-the-studio" album purporting to be the soundtrack of a real Beach Boys party!

As with most modest proposals, it had the genius of simplicity; camped in Western Studios for four days in September, the band ran through their own personal favourites (and dismantled two of their own classics) accompanied solely by acoustic guitars, bongos and bass, the tapes rolling ceaselessly. It could be credibly argued that the result – before the 'party' effects (taped at a real gathering at Love's house) were added – was the world's first "Unplugged" album, and was certainly a dazzling showcase for the band's vocal expertise. In buying time for 'Pet Sounds', it was

100% successful; as an enjoyable album in its own right, it was reasonably worthwhile... and it was the last original Beach Boys US Top Ten album for nearly eleven years, perhaps because from this point on, Beach Boys albums appealed more to grown-ups and far less to teenagers... In the UK, it was their second chart album and first to reach the Top 3.

(BABY) HULLY GULLY
(Smith/Goldsmith)

Previously a very small 1960 hit for black Los Angeles-based doowop quartet The Olympics (best known for their 1958 hit, 'Western Movies'), and just one of numerous cover versions on 'Party'!. Love takes the lead vocal, but the true gem is the band chorus.

I SHOULD HAVE KNOWN BETTER
(Lennon/McCartney)

Johnston on bongos, Carl Wilson & Jardine on lead vocals, on this cover of a Beatles song from *A Hard Day's Night* best described as amusing chaos.

TELL ME WHY
(Lennon/McCartney)

The same cast as above on another *Hard Day's Night* film song, but this time in somewhat tighter form.

PAPA-OOM-MOW-MOW
(Frazier/White/Harris/ Wilson)

Having evidently learnt nothing from the previous year's live LP, Love and Brian Wilson once more attempt vocal suicide. Perhaps The Beach Boys knew The Rivingtons – why else would any non-garage band cover this repetitive item twice?

MOUNTAIN OF LOVE
(Dorman)

Out-takes reveal that the released version by The Beach Boys of the Johnny Rivers 1964 US Top 10 hit is actually something like take 13. Love's vocal fronts an excellent carbon copy of this obvious hit written by Mississippi-born Harold Dorman, whose original version all but reached the US Top 20 in 1960.

DEVOTED TO YOU
(Bryant)

Credited to The Cleverly Brothers on the sleeve, Love & Brian Wilson team up to good effect on this 1958 Everly Brothers standard. The highlight of the album, some cynics consider this track too polished to be truly 'live'.

ALLEY OOP
(Frazier)

A 1960 US Number One hit for The Hollywood Argyles (alias Gary Paxton of Skip & Flip, a duo in which his partner was Skip Battin, later of The Byrds). Love leads The Beach Boys in a reprise of their 'Hully Gully' style.

YOU'VE GOT TO HIDE YOUR LOVE AWAY
(Lennon/McCartney)

Dennis Wilson provides an unexpected highlight on yet another cover of a film song by The Beatles, this time from *Help!*, which remained a live Beach Boys staple into 1966.

THERE'S NO OTHER (LIKE MY BABY)
(Spector/Bates)

It was inevitable that a Phil Spector song would be included on 'Party!', and the chorus vocal on this cover of the début US hit by The Crystals packs a punch behind Brian Wilson's clear lead.

I GET AROUND/LITTLE DEUCE COUPE
(B.Wilson/Love*- B.Wilson/Christian)

... or how to destroy your career in two easy lessons. A splendid time is had by all, to the detriment of two classics. Great stuff.

THE TIMES THEY ARE A-CHANGIN'
(Dylan)

Jardine, the group's token folkie, gets his chance to shine on this cover of the title track of Bob Dylan's classic third LP, and is resolutely upstaged by everyone else. Probably not his favourite moment of Beach Boys history.

BARBARA ANN
(Fassert)

Escaping from a Jan & Dean session down the hallway, Dean Torrence stuck his head into Western Studio 3 at a time when the "Boys" had run out of songs to destroy/cover, and suggested they tackle this 1961 US Top 20 hit by Bronx band The Regents. He wound up singing lead with

Brian Wilson on a track released as an edited 45, which became the first UK Top 3 hit for The Beach Boys, and their fifth US Top 3 single. Listen for Carl Wilson's verbal credit – for contractual reasons, Torrence, who was then signed to Liberty Records, could not be credited on the album.

The Beach Boys Pet Sounds

Sloop John B./Caroline No
Wouldn't It Be Nice/You Still Believe In Me
That's Not Me/Don't Talk (Put Your Head on My Shoulder)
I'm Waiting For The Day/Let's Go Away For Awhile
God Only Knows/I Know There's An Answer/Here Today
I Just Wasn't Made For These Times/Pet Sounds

PET SOUNDS

(CAPITOL T 2458 [LP] CDP 7 48421 2 [CD]; RELEASED MAY 1966)

Having bought time (and handed Capitol a purely incidental hit album) with 'Party!', Brian Wilson now turned his full attention to his new project. Inspired by The Beatles' 'Rubber Soul' LP, which he considered to be "full of all good stuff, no filler", he told wife Marilyn: "I'm gonna make the best rock album in the world"... and, in the view of many expert critics, succeeded. In three Nineties UK polls, 'Pet Sounds' has emerged at or near the top of the pile each time – and these are critics' polls, the considered opinion of professional rock journalists, and not merely a reflection of the current flavour of the month. An artistic validation thirty years too late, true, but very welcome all the same.

Brian's compositional style for 'Pet Sounds' bordered on the impressionistic; rather than writing a complete melody, he instead sketched out what he called "feels... specific rhythm patterns, fragments of ideas". The melody and lyric would come later, inspired directly by the mood of the "feels". As a writing method, it was luxurious, organic... and time consuming, to the extent that, when Capitol reminded Wilson that a 'proper' LP was again overdue, just one song had been completed ('Sloop John B', not a candidate for the LP in Brian's mind) and one basic track recorded ('In My Childhood' – which he decided he hated). Gripped by a mild panic, and with the band away on tour, he recalled a chance acquaintance, advertising jingle writer Tony Asher, whom he asked to help out with lyrics. Asher immediately agreed, but soon found out that collaborating with Wilson (whose chemical experimentation was escalating) was a distinct chore outside the strictly musical arena, and in later years offered the famous quote that Brian Wilson was "a genius musician, but an amateur human being".

The Beach Boys, largely absent on tour while their resident Svengali was creating, offered a more considered, if fragmented, critical opinion. Dennis and Carl Wilson loved the new music; Jardine decided "it sure doesn't sound like the old stuff"; and Love was memorably forthright – "don't fuck with the formula"; (Johnston also loved the music, but as a wage slave like Jardine – rather than a voting member of the corporation – had no real clout in such matters). Love's disapproval also concerned certain lyrical themes which Brian, ever diplomatic, duly ensured were revised. In other matters, however, Wilson was totally intransigent, and this benign dictatorship resulted in 'Pet Sounds' being, essentially, a Brian Wilson solo album with guest vocalists. None of the rest of the band contributed instrumentally, and there is strong documentary evidence that, after group vocal sessions, Wilson would return alone to the studio and re-record them his way; which is not to imply that vocals by his colleagues were in any way substandard, but rather was an example of his increasingly perfectionist nature (something that session musicians were already well aware of). As was his habit, he spent much

longer in the studio than Capitol deemed fit, with the result that, apart from the previously released 'Sloop John B' and 'Caroline, No', all of 'Pet Sounds'' complex backing tracks and vocals were mixed in a single nine-hour session (which probably explains the chatter heard on some tracks).

'Pet Sounds' has been called an early concept album; while all the main participants repeatedly deny this, it is not difficult to discern a uniting theme – of hopes and aspirations dashed, of a search for love doomed to failure – and even, some claim, by judicious reprogramming of the CD track order, to produce a coherent storyline tracing the rise and fall of a relationship... and certainly the pervading air of 'Pet Sounds' is one of gentle melancholy. Perhaps that's why, even though it included three US Top 40 hits, 'Pet Sounds' sold significantly fewer copies than any Beach Boys LP since 'Surfin' Safari' and only just made the US Top 10, although it was a major commercial success in Britain, where it became their first Top 10 LP and their first to spend over six months in the chart.

Artistically, however, it was a different story: the music business understood that something very special indeed was happening in Southern California, and Brian suddenly found himself at the vanguard of the nascent pop revolution, regarded as an innovator, a man with something to say of whom much was expected. Fortunately, the next step was already well in hand: during the 'Pet Sounds' sessions, Wilson had also taken a couple of stabs at another title – 'Good Vibrations'.

It had been the intention of Capitol Records to mark the 30th Anniversary of the release of 'Pet Sounds' with a revolutionary 4 CD box set comprising a remastered mono version (using HD/CD technology), session material as per the fifth CD of the 'Good Vibrations' box set (including the first ever 'Good Vibrations' session), the instrumental and vocal tracks in isolation (and stereo!) and, at long last, the first true stereo mix of the complete album. This was lovingly and excellently constructed by Mark Linnett, using the original instrumental four track and vocal eight track session tapes. Synchronisation was possible because once he was satisfied with the instrumental backing, Brian Wilson had mixed it down to mono on one of the eight tracks on the eight track tape, leaving seven tracks for vocals. Linnett thus was able to work with what were effectively 11 tracks for each song once he had synchronised the start of the instrumental four track with the mixed down mono instrumental track. Well, that's how it has been explained. The results were stunning, opening up new windows on each song, and the deconstructed vocal and instrumental versions not only allowed intimate study of Brian Wilson's working methods (as did the session tapes, which were also in stereo), but also confirmed that the majority of the vocals on the album were (as had long been rumoured) by Brian Wilson. Whether or not this rankled with the rest of the group is not known, but the fact is that the boxed set had been approved by Brian Wilson and scheduled for a May 1996 release but was postponed several times; once because the band wanted the booklet(s) re-written, and on another occasion because they demanded the stereo mix be done again.

At the time of writing, the 'Pet Sounds' box set is scheduled for release in late 1996 or early 1997.

WOULDN'T IT BE NICE
(B.Wilson/Asher/Love*)

Recorded at Gold Star Studios (where many of Phil Spector's masterpieces were created), this classic US Top 10 hit's lilting guitar intro and explosive drum shot usher in a bitter-sweet tale of longings as yet unfulfilled, hopes tempered by reality. An accordion-driven track of impressive complexity overlaid with Brian Wilson's keen lead and Love's wonderfully mellow middle-eight vocal, cushioned by sumptuous group harmonies, the lyrical hints at immorality in the first two verses are allayed by the matrimonial hopes of the bridge.

A 24-carat masterpiece, this was brain-lessly released in Britain as the flip side of the Top 3 'God Only Knows' single; a classic case of losing an obvious hit through bad judge-ment – in the US, 'God Only Knows' was the flip side of 'Wouldn't It Be Nice ', but in Britain, 'God Only Knows' was the favoured track on pirate radio and thus became a smash hit. Included on the boxed set collectors' CD in vocal split format, the vocals are even more stunning... and curiously, it's Brian and not Mike singing the middle-eight.

YOU STILL BELIEVE IN ME
(B.Wilson/Asher)

The odd bicycle bell and horn interjections in this stately, almost hymn-like number are relics of the song's original incarnation as 'In My Childhood', a number which Wilson aban-doned, but which had been recorded in such a way that these extraneous sounds could not be erased when he decided to recycle the track... yet strangely, they still fit. Brian's lead vocal is sweetness personified, and the cho-rus harmony blocks are truly angelic. The bell-like piano intro was achieved by plucking the strings of the instrument, and apparently required extensive practise!

THAT'S NOT ME
(B.Wilson/Asher)

The eccentric drum patterns underpinning this track heighten the sense of uncertainty evi-dent in the lyric, whilst a melodic bass line weaves in and around Love's questioning vocal and Brian Wilson's plaintive counter. As spellbinding, in the view of some commenta-tors, as the two previous tracks.

DON'T TALK (PUT YOUR HEAD ON MY SHOULDER)
(B.Wilson/Asher)

The last track recorded for the album, and a solo vocal performance from Brian Wilson, this languid confection is one of his most romantic compositions and, according to some critics, exudes almost overwhelming emotion.

I'M WAITING FOR THE DAY
(B.Wilson/Love)

An attention-grabbing timpani intro leads into a track of great contrasts, juxtaposing reflective passages with aggressive verses to great effect. Similarly, Brian Wilson's lead vocal swings from tender to strident as required. Originally written in 1964 and credited to Wilson alone, Love's compositional contribution was apparently to amend eight words.

LET'S GO AWAY FOR A WHILE
(B.Wilson)

A year after the release of 'Pet Sounds', Brian Wilson considered this wistfully atmospheric track to be "the most satisfying piece of music I've ever made", a statement with which many Beach Boys fans and commentators would concur. Although presented as an instrumental, and long thought to have been conceived as such – even though lyrics were written by Asher – it emerged in 1995 that a session for vocals was scheduled, but – at Capitol's insistence – was used instead to mix the album. The story goes that as part of a running joke then current, the song was semi-seriously called 'Let's Go Away For A While (And Then We'll Have World Peace)'

SLOOP JOHN B.
(Trad. arr. B.Wilson)

Released in March, 1966, as a single which was a Top 3 hit on both sides of the Atlantic, this version of a traditional folk song (a 1960 UK hit for Lonnie Donegan as 'I Wanna Go Home') was recorded in late 1965 at Jardine's instigation, although the arrangement is 100% Brian Wilson. The sore thumb of the album in lyrical terms, it was never intended for this LP until Capitol's insistence that including a recent hit made commercial sense. Even so, it's a compelling vocal performance, especially during the a cappella break. Love and Wilson share lead vocals.

GOD ONLY KNOWS
(B.Wilson/Asher)

Possibly Carl Wilson's crowning vocal achievement, this has been described by one noted Beach Boys historian as the most beautiful suicide song ever (presumably on the strength of the lines "The world would show nothing to me, So what good would living do me?"). Be that as it may, Carl's honeyed lead is matched by a shimmering backing track and a gorgeous rotating tag featuring Brian Wilson and Johnston. A US Top 40 hit as the B-side to 'Wouldn't It Be Nice?' and a UK Top 3 smash (see above), Brian reputedly had some misgivings about including the word "God" in the song title; Asher successfully talked him round.

A major highlight of the 1993 'Good Vibrations' boxed set was a nine minute session track, illustrating the importance of the studio musicians in developing the song, and culminating with a version featuring not only Brian's original guide vocal but also an awesome and previously unheard vocal tag of immense complexity and beauty. Why this was consigned to the vaults remains a complete mystery.

I KNOW THERE'S AN ANSWER
(B.Wilson/Asher/Sachen/ Love*)

Initially written and recorded as 'Hang On To Your Ego', this was the item that sent Love's blood pressure soaring, and caused Brian Wilson to get road manager Terry Sachen to marginally revise the lyrics. The track is driven nicely by bass harmonica and banjo, and to many fans, the voice on the verse after Love's first line sounds awfully like Jardine rather than Brian.

HERE TODAY
(B.Wilson/Asher)

A cascading bass line into the chorus and the mid-song chatter highlight this forceful song taken from an ex-boyfriend's point of view. If the chords behind the verse sound familiar,

they should – Brian Wilson recycled the progression in 'Good Vibrations'. Love is spot on as usual. The instrumental track was recorded at Sunset Sound.

I JUST WASN'T MADE FOR THESE TIMES
(B.Wilson/Asher)

A less-than-subtle *cri de coeur* from Brian Wilson, this solo performance boasts what may be the first ever use on a rock song of a thérémin (a strange instrument, to say the least, later used extensively on 'Good Vibrations'), probably played by Paul Tanner. The three part vocal chorus has attracted great attention as the second and third lines are less than clear; session tapes reveal them to be "Ain't found the one thing I can put my heart and soul into" and "My friends don't know (or want) me". The instrumental track was recorded at Gold Star.

PET SOUNDS
(B.Wilson)

'Sloop John B' aside, this spiky instrumental was long thought to be the first track recorded for 'Pet Sounds' (further research has since disproved the notion), and was originally called 'Run, James, Run' (the James in question reportedly being Bond, as in 007).

CAROLINE, NO
(B.Wilson/Asher)

Ushered in by drummer Hal Blaine tapping on an empty soda syphon bottle, this bitter-sweet US Top 40 ballad was issued as a Brian Wilson solo single. As with 'Surfin'', father Murry Wilson insisted the master be sped up a tone to make Brian sound younger. The barking on the tag was supplied by Brian's dogs at the time, Banana (a beagle) and Louie (a weimaraner).

UNRELEASED BACKGROUNDS+
(B.Wilson)

... to 'Don't Talk': probably a wise omission from the LP in 1966.

HANG ON TO YOUR EGO+
(B.Wilson/Asher)

Brian Wilson handles the original lyric in a working vocal over a slightly incomplete track. Some find it difficult to understand precisely what Love found so objectionable. Brian Wilson's appeal to engineer Chuck Britz at the end is priceless, as is the latter's response. As with 'God Only Knows', the boxed set included enlightening session material of this title, as well as an alternate version.

TROMBONE DIXIE+
(B.Wilson)

According to David Leaf's excellent 'Pet Sounds' CD booklet, it says 'Trombone Dixie' on the tape box and features a trombone, so that'll have to do. Reprising (among others) a riff from 'The Little Girl I Once Knew', Brian Wilson would later recycle part of this perky instrumental into 'Had To Phone Ya' on '15 Big Ones', the group's 1976 comeback LP.

SMiLE

Brother records

SMILE

(CAPITOL T 2580 [LP]; NOT RELEASED)

Never completed, 'Smile', or the period during which sessions for an album to be called 'Smile' were held, is the pivotal moment in the history of both The Beach Boys (musically) and of Brian Wilson (creatively and personally), for the roots of just about every ill later to beset the band and their leading light can be traced to this ten-month period of towering creativity, eventually brought to a crashing halt by indulgence, excess, resentment, misunderstanding, paranoia and plain old-fashioned stupidity.

'Smile' remains rock's only bona fide mystery, despite a steady, if fragmentary, stream of information and music coming to light over the years, climaxing with the half-hour of original session material included on the 1993 boxed set. This abiding enigma is due to one simple fact: only Brian Wilson ever knew exactly how 'Smile' was going to be constituted, and it's possible that, back in 1966/7, even he wasn't too sure. The back of the 'Smile' sleeve (which does exist) listed twelve titles, accompanied by the cryptic note, "see label for correct playing order", indicating at the very least that he hadn't settled on a satisfactory sequence by late 1966. From the surviving material, one thing is certain: even by the standards of the time, it would have been a very eclectic, supremely hip, and possibly totally uncommercial, record. We'll never know.

Discounting 'Good Vibrations', from August 1966 to mid-May 1967, Brian held nearly eighty sessions for some eighteen titles, resulting in songs in varying stages of completion ('Wonderful' was almost complete, 'The Elements' fragmentary). Doubtless under pressure from Capitol, he had submitted a track listing containing the following titles:'Do You Like Worms'/'Wind Chimes'/'Heroes And Villains'/'Surf's Up'/'Good Vibrations'/'Cabin Essence'/'Wonderful'/'I'm In Great Shape'/'Child Is

Father To the Man'/'The Elements'/'Vega-Tables'/'The Old Master Painter'. Given prevailing conditions, not to mention Brian's state of mind (this was the era of the famous "piano-in-the-sandbox" episode: Brian felt he would be inspired by sand between his toes, but didn't want to actually go to the beach... so he had several tons of sand dumped in his front room, much to the delight of Banana and Louie), that was probably how he saw the album at that precise moment – the next day, the list might have been totally different.

Compositionally, if not musically, 'Smile' was a direct evolution from 'Pet Sounds' via 'Good Vibrations'; with 'Vibes', Brian took his "feels" method of composition and further refined it by recording those "feels" and then assembling them into a song... and when it worked, he saw no reason why a whole album couldn't be similarly constructed. And he came awfully close to pulling it off. Fans have tried to explain the non-appearance of 'Smile' by citing excessive drug usage, severe resistance from other band members, legal disputes with Capitol, the appearance of 'Sgt. Pepper',

and so on. Certainly, Brian's chemical ingestion during the 'Smile' sessions was alarming, even compared with his previous usage, but worse was to come... and yes, there were problems with certain group members on the band's return from a European tour – but to blame the collapse of 'Smile' totally on this ignores the fact that such experimental songs as 'Cabin Essence' had already been attempted before the tour. A more recent notion is that 'Smile' fell foul of Brian's own essentially good nature. Ever eager to please, he just couldn't bring himself to tell the others what had been becoming evident to him for some time – he'd lost the plot, didn't know how or where all the bits were supposed to fit... in short, he couldn't do it. It's as neat a solution as any other, and who knows, it may even be the truth; no-one will ever know. Inevitably, of course, 'Smile' fell apart anyway when Brian did.

(The titles described below were all originally intended to be included on 'Smile', and are dealt with in approximate order of recording.)

GOOD VIBRATIONS
(B.Wilson/Love)

Brian Wilson originally began recording 'Good Vibrations' during the 'Pet Sounds' sessions, and returned to his "pocket symphony" during the summer of 1966. Recorded at three studios in eight sessions over six months, he distilled three and a half minutes of pure aural magic from a reported 90 hours of tape, assembling and discarding at least three completed versions before settling on one that topped charts world-wide. Two prototypes can be heard on the 1983 'Rarities' album (lacking only the lead vocal) and on the 1993 boxed set (the so-called "Wilson Pickett" version – Brian considered selling the song to Pickett's label – with what may well be Tony Asher's original lyric), which also contains over eight minutes of discarded fragments, a very early live version and the instrumental track of the released version in stereo.

Revolutionary in its modular structure, use of cello as a rhythm instrument (played by Jesse Erlich and suggested by Van Dyke Parks, who declined a request to supply new lyrics) and its use of the thérémin, it was Brian's satisfaction with this song that gave him the confidence to attempt 'Smile', having proved that a collage method of composition was feasible. The moving harmonies have never been bettered, Carl Wilson's lead vocal (with Brian hitting the highs in the verse) is perfect – in short a magical track. The song's inclusion on 'Smile', and later on 'Smiley Smile', was Capitol's idea.

WIND CHIMES
(B.Wilson)

As presented on the 1993 boxed set, the original 'Wind Chimes' is Brian's rough edit of three contrasting sections – Carl's sweet lead over a quietly humorous marimba, a muscular group vocal and a piano tag that sounds not unlike 'Can't Wait Too Long' – making for one of 'Smile's less involved songs. The less forceful version re-recorded for 'Smiley Smile' featured a vocal handed from member to member over a melody so free-form as to be almost intermittent. The influence of the dreaded weed is all too evident... yet, the delicate, almost inaudible tag is truly charming. Van Dyke Parks reportedly helped with the lyrics.

WONDERFUL
(B.Wilson/Parks)

This subtle variation on the 'Heroes And Villains' chorus melody (or did this come first?) is heartbreaking in its delicate fragility, perfectly complemented by Brian's crystalline vocal. As recut for 'Smiley Smile', Carl Wilson's intimate – if slightly mellow – lead almost makes sense of Parks' cryptic lyric... and deciphering the chatter during the strange mid-song break has long been a challenge to fans ("Don't you think you're God-vibrations... let's go for the record" are allegedly audible).

OUR PRAYER
(B.Wilson)

An exquisite a cappella exercise in celestial wordless harmony. The version released on '20/20' is basically the 'Smile' recording with a few additional 1968 overdubs.

CABIN ESSENCE
(B.Wilson/Parks)

A dazzling synthesis of contrasting musical styles and brilliantly counterpointed by Van Dyke Parks' impressionistic lyrics, 'Cabin Essence', more than any other relic, hints at the lost majesty of 'Smile'. The version released on '20/20' had only Carl's vocal added. A highlight of the 1993 5CD box set is the instrumental track, an excellent argument for the 'Brian Wilson is a genius' theory. Stripped of the (admittedly wondrous) vocals, it is simply breathtaking.

CHILD IS FATHER TO THE MAN
(B.Wilson)

The version stapled onto the end of 'Surf's Up' is a complete 1971 re-recording of yet another variation of the so-called 'Bicycle Rider'/'Heroes And Villains' theme. The original remains hauntingly incomplete.

DO YOU LIKE WORMS?
(B.Wilson)

Easily the most experimental of all the 'Smile' material, yet once again developed from the same 'Heroes And Villains' riff as 'Wonderful' and 'Child', the structure of 'Worms' owed nothing to anything that had gone before (or since), and yet manages to attain a degree of coherence whilst remaining resolutely free-form. The disparate elements of pounding tim-pani, music-box harpsichord, loosely Hawaiian instrumentation and silky-smooth group vocals are never less than compelling, while the lyric, such as it is, enhances the mood without once making the slightest sense...

SURF'S UP
(B.Wilson/Parks)

Mythical in its inaccessibility, the inclusion on 'Surf's Up' of this long-lost 'Smile' jewel qui-etly ignores the fact that not only did Brian Wilson not want the track released, but also that what we hear is a 1971 creation (admit-tedly mostly from original 'Smile' material). Brian's section comes from an unused 1967 CBS TV session (the complete version is available on the 1993 boxed set) whilst brother Carl's impeccable vocal is dubbed over an instrumental track also from 1967 (similarly released on the boxed set). The final choral section is a reworked 'Smile' track orig-inally entitled 'Child Is Father To the Man'...

yet even in this hybrid form, the legend that had grown around the song since its sole TV airing in 1967 was seen to have been justified. Parks' translucent lyric complements to per-fection an instrumental track of delicate beauty to achieve something approaching a rock hymn. Magical.

THE ELEMENTS – MRS. O'LEARY'S COW (FIRE)
(B.Wilson)

That 'Fire', as it's popularly tagged, was accorded an official (albeit partial) release as part of the 1985 video biography of The Beach Boys, 'An American Band', is one of rock's better kept secrets. The November session that produced the existing version has often been nominated as the point where Brian Wilson's eccentricity finally descended into true paranoia, and his continuing dislike of even discussing the episode would appear to confirm such a view: Brian insisted that all the musicians involved must wear fireman's hel-mets, and quite coincidentally (although not in his opinion), the building across the street from the studio burned down very shortly afterwards. Brian's altered perception regarded this as an omen, and that the fire had resulted from his music... The track itself (titled for the animal allegedly responsible for the Great Chicago Fire of 1871) stands alone in Beach Boys history as a disturbingly powerful and successful example of pictorial music, the strings, bass, guitars and percussion melding to paint a graphic scene of destruction.

HEROES AND VILLAINS
(B.Wilson/Parks)

Brian Wilson devoted more time to this song than to any other of the 'Smile' material, and the chorus melody may have been intended as the underlying musical thread unifying the album, as it crops up in several other songs, most notably 'Wonderful'. The version eventually released in 1967 comprised parts of the original 'Smile' recordings married with later revisions, a seemingly wilful act of spite, as many of the discarded sections contained what journalist Jules Seigal referred to at the time as "sequences of extraordinary power and beauty". Nonetheless, what remains is a

dazzling vocal display, and an excellent example of how Brian constructed the 'Smile' songs out of diverse melodic fragments. That such an experimental work could be released as a single and still go US Top 20/UK Top 10, hints at the possibilities lost.

Wilson's handling of Parks' elliptical lyric – which purportedly concerns Brian's battle with Capitol as much as it addresses the Old West – is surefooted, and the band toss off the incredibly complex vocals with a confidence born of familiarity. In 1990, an alternate version – including the long-lost "cantina" section – emerged on the 'Smiley Smile'/'Wild Honey' Twofer. Later, the 1993 boxed set included some ten minutes of 'H&V' discards, notably the majority of 'Heroes And Villains Pt. 2' – the final four minutes of the 'H&V (sections)' track (except that the last sixty seconds doesn't belong there...). The latter was the intended B-side of a projected 'H&V' single and a title which gave rise to one of the more enduring 'Smile' myths, that of the existence of a version of 'H&V' lasting some seven minutes. Evidently some bright spark saw a Capitol 45 release sheet listing of 'Heroes And Villains/Heroes And Villains Pt. 2' and jumped to the conclusion that it must be a single song spread over two sides of a 45, a classic example of 2+2 = 5.

The boxed set also included a track entitled 'Heroes And Villains (intro)', actually a bells and whistles rendition of the main Fire Music melody – make of that what you will. Similarly, the "cantina" version of 'H&V' had fifty seconds of an unused 'Heroes' section tacked onto the end, a move that many 'Smile' aficionados doubt Brian Wilson approved – it just sounds wrong.

released on 'Smiley Smile' and subtly retitled (as 'Vegetables' - sic) was another hybrid of 'Smile' material and hastily re-recorded stuff, and was at one time set to be the follow-up to 'Heroes And Villains'.

Parks' lyric is as straightforward as he ever gets, and on both sections the group vocals are excellent (the 'Smile' section starts at 1.30 into the song, and features Brian Wilson and Alan Jardine on lead), yet even in the "anything goes" ambience of the mid-Sixties, the song is resolutely uncommercial.

VEGA-TABLES
(B.Wilson/Parks)

Two further myths require demolishing: 'Vega-Tables' never was the Earth section of 'The Elements', nor did Paul McCartney either play on or co-produce this, or any other version. The boxed set includes an original 'Smile' recording – though obviously not the master take – complete with 'Mama Says' popping up in the middle, and it's a whole bunch of fun (though it must be noted that the last forty seconds isn't 'Vega-Tables' at all but rather an unused section of 'Wonderful'). The version

THE ELEMENTS – LOVE TO SAY DA-DA (WATER)
(B.Wilson)

Until a thin clarinet line gives the game away, this distant ancestor of 'Sunflower''s 'Cool Cool Water' remains anonymous in the extreme. Recorded at the tail-end of the 'Smile' sessions in May 1967, the fragmentary nature of this title accurately reflected the state of not only Brian Wilson's mind, but also of The Beach Boys themselves.

SMILEY SMILE

(BROTHER 9001 [LP] CDP 7 93696 2 [CD];
RELEASED SEPTEMBER 1967)

The release of 'Smiley Smile' completed one of the most dramatic falls from grace the world of rock'n'roll has ever seen. As 1967 dawned, Brian Wilson & The Beach Boys seemed on the verge of a future whose possibilities appeared limitless – 'Good Vibrations' was topping charts worldwide, in a year-end poll in New Musical Express, they just shaded the Beatles for Top World Group honours... and the word was that Wilson was creating a new album – 'Smile' – that would be the definitive statement of the emerging psychedelic counter-culture. Nine months later, everything lay in ruins and the advent of 'Sgt. Pepper' by The Beatles notwithstanding, the primary reason was the non-appearance of 'Smile', and the eventual release of 'Smiley Smile', easily the most bizarre – and disappointing – album by a major act during the Sixties.

Even after the announcement in May, 1967 of 'Smile's' abandonment, it was reasonable to assume that any replacement LP would continue the process initiated by 'Pet Sounds'; hence the stunned reception accorded 'Smiley Smile', for, the two previously released tracks aside, the word "basic" didn't even come close to describing the utter simplicity of the songs and performances. It was the first album to carry the credit "Produced By The Beach Boys"... but the truth was it wasn't so much produced as merely recorded, and as it later emerged, the reason why was simple – most of the band were heavily into chemical experimentation at the time, and this was the best they could manage. That their vocal prowess emerged from the haze largely undimmed is amazing... that Capitol agreed to even distribute 'Smiley Smile', released on the band's own Brother Records label, is all the more astonishing. The LP was not a great commercial success, just failing to make the US Top 40 during a five month chart residency, and barely making the Top 10 during a brief visit to the UK chart.

HEROES AND VILLAINS
(B.Wilson/Parks)

See 'Smile' album.

VEGE-TABLES
(B.Wilson/Parks)

See 'Smile' album.

FALL BREAKS AND BACK TO WINTER (WOODY WOODPECKER SYMPHONY)
(B.Wilson)

This haunting instrumental is considered by some Beach Boys historians to be the remnants of the Earth Music from 'Smile''s 'The Elements' suite, and certainly the harmonies and bass are very like the basic chords to 'Mrs O'Leary's Cow', better known as the Fire Music... but no-one really knows.

SHE'S GOIN' BALD
(B.Wilson/Love/Parks)

Originally cut during the 'Smile' sessions as 'He Writes Speeches', this terminally bizarre yet strangely enjoyable song gives just about everyone a line to sing – or declaim – during a number that must have given Mike Love pause for thought. Mixed way back under the first section is a 'Heroes And Villains' chant, and the speeded-up middle eight is based on

'Get A Job', the 1958 US Number One by Philadelphia doo-wop quartet, The Silhouettes.

LITTLE PAD
(B.Wilson)

Cotton candy-sweet vocals from the band, a gentle lead from Carl Wilson and yes, they all sound as high as kites.

GOOD VIBRATIONS
(B.Wilson/Love)

See 'Smile' album.

WITH ME TONIGHT
(B.Wilson)

Another of the circular chants that epitomised 'Smiley Smile', with lead vocalist Carl Wilson again in mellow voice; the basso profondo "GOOD!" belongs to Arnie Geller, Brian Wilson's assistant at that time. A much more complex and heavily produced version of this pops up unexpectedly in the middle of a 'Heroes And Villains' fragment...

WIND CHIMES
(B.Wilson)

See 'Smile' album.

GETTIN' HUNGRY
(B.Wilson/Love)

When this stop-start little rocker was released as an unsuccessful 45, it was credited not to The Beach Boys, but as by Brian & Mike (sic). A slightly more substantial song than most on the album.

WONDERFUL
(B.Wilson/Parks)

See 'Smile' album.

WHISTLE IN
(B.Wilson)

Reprising a melody line from 'Smile''s 'Do You Like Worms?', this circular mantra ended the original vinyl album. Carl Wilson and Love split vocal chores.

HEROES AND VILLAINS+
(ALTERNATE VERSION)
(B.Wilson/Parks)

See 'Smile' album.

GOOD VIBRATIONS+
(SESSIONS)
(B.Wilson)

See 'Smile' album.

GOOD VIBRATIONS+
(EARLY VERSION)
(B.Wilson/Asher)

See 'Smile' album.

YOU'RE WELCOME+
(B.Wilson)

The B-side of the 'Heroes And Villains' single, this Brian Wilson solo performance was recorded during the 'Smile' sessions.

THEIR HEARTS WERE FULL OF SPRING+
(Troup)

Written by the man also responsible for both 'Route 66' and 'The Girl Can't Help It' (among many standards), this was recorded at rehearsals for the 1967 Hawaii concerts, and the vocal wizardry shines through untarnished by what was by then, considerable use of "substances".

WILD HONEY
(CAPITOL T 2859 [LP] CDP 7 93696 2 [CD];
RELEASED DECEMBER 1967)

"Wild Honey' was music for Brian to cool out by" was Carl Wilson's view of the second original Beach Boys LP of 1967, and it's hard to disagree. 'Smiley Smile', tinged with the grand failure of 'Smile', was the result of a desperate need to come up with some – any – product, but 'Wild Honey' was in many ways the first Beach Boys reunion album, as for the first time since 'Surfer Girl', the band themselves played the majority of the instruments on an album. And, just as previous LPs had reflected Brian Wilson's current preoccupations, so 'Wild Honey' documented a new, simpler lifestyle – indeed, its title was inspired by an item from the kitchen cupboard.

However, although the US chart placing (Top 30) was notably better than that achieved by 'Smiley Smile', the sales were even lower, and obviously, times were changing, Mike Love later observing that the band "paid its dues after we became

famous". However, its UK chart life and peak position in the Top 10 both improved on 'Smiley Smile''s performance.

'Wild Honey' was originally scheduled for release with a somewhat different running order (including an early version of 'Cool, Cool Water') on the Brother Records label (Brother 9003). From evidence unearthed by 'Smile' researcher/surf music historian Domenic Priore, it seems likely that Brother 9002 was intended, by Capitol at least, to be a 10 track 'Smile' album.

WILD HONEY
(B.Wilson/Love)

The third Beach Boys song to feature a thérémin, this track starkly posted the album's ambitions: basic band instrumentation, bare production (again credited to The Beach Boys) and decidedly rough and ready harmonies. At least it was a proper song, and though Dennis Wilson's bass drum was apparently recorded from the hallway (as with most of 'Smiley Smile', the whole album was recorded at Brian Wilson's house), Carl Wilson turns in a spirited lead vocal. As a single, it went US Top 40, and briefly UK Top 30.

AREN'T YOU GLAD
(B.Wilson/Love)

Co-writers Love and Brian Wilson deftly handle the leads on this perky little item, underscored by some neat horn lines.

I WAS MADE TO LOVE HER
(Cosby/Hardaway/Moy/Wonder)

One of the more densely produced tracks on 'Wild Honey' (a relative judgement), this cover of the Stevie Wonder standard which had been a massive international hit six months earlier finds Carl Wilson contributing a somewhat strained lead vocal. An alternate version, with an a cappella break, was released on Capitol's 1983 'Rarities' album.

COUNTRY AIR
(B.Wilson/Love)

Strong harmonies on the chorus make this one of the album's highlights. Some maintain that this is an expansion of the Air music from 'Smile''s 'The Elements'.

A THING OR TWO
(B.Wilson/Love)

Harking back to 'Smiley Smile' with its two-part structure, this loose rocker slopes along without any great conviction. Love and Brian Wilson (or is it Carl ?) turn in workmanlike vocals.

DARLIN'
(B.Wilson/Love)

Easily the most fully realised track on the album, 'Darlin'' evolved from a 1963 Brian Wilson production of 'Thinkin'' 'Bout You Baby' for Sharon Marie, and was originally intended for Redwood, a band signed by Wilson to Brother Records. According to Danny Hutton, lead singer of Redwood, the rest of The Beach Boys heard Wilson's backing track and promptly appropriated it for themselves. (Redwood later evolved into the hugely successful Three Dog Night, a group which accumulated a dozen gold albums between 1969 and 1974.) Carl Wilson's strong lead vocal, plus excellent group harmonies, helped the 45 just crack the US Top 20, and almost make the UK Top 10.

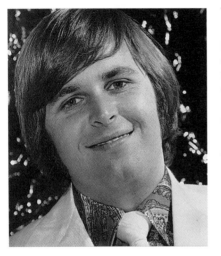

HERE COMES THE NIGHT
(B.Wilson/Love)

Redeemed by gritty backing vocals – mixed slightly too low – this otherwise inoffensive number would be resurrected in 1979 as a disco-styled remake.

LET THE WIND BLOW
(B.Wilson/Love)

Written mostly by Love, and rearranged by Brian Wilson, this is the album's hidden gem. Both composers contribute vocals of sweetness and strength to this waltz-styled ballad.

HOW SHE BOOGALOOED IT
(Love/Johnston/Jardine/ C.Wilson)

This frenetic cut hasn't really aged well – "S-O-C-K-I-T to me" indeed – and Jardine was to come up with far better vocals... but note the absence of B.Wilson on the writing credits.

I'D LOVE JUST ONCE TO SEE YOU
(B.Wilson/Love)

An early example of Brian Wilson's "slice-of-life" compositions, the very inconsequentiality of this song charms, as does the mildly risqué tag. A "matter of fact" vocal from the composer.

MAMA SAYS
(B.Wilson/Love)

It's almost as if the band were saving all the vocals for this wonderful slab of harmony, a 'Smile' composition originally a part of 'Vega-Tables'.

CAN'T WAIT TOO LONG+
(B.Wilson)

An edit (not by Brian Wilson) of sections recorded during the 'Wild Honey' and '20/20' sessions – and thus not a 'Smile' song, as was once assumed – this shimmering example of repetition elevated to an art form shows just what Brian could still deliver, should he set his mind to it. An alternate version released on the 1993 boxed set features additional vocal lines. Simply magnificent.

FRIENDS
(CAPITOL ST 2895 [LP] CDP 7 93697 2 [CD]; RELEASED JUNE 1968)

Looking back on Beach Boys LPs of the late Sixties, there's been a trend among critics to assign an overall label to each album from that era – 'Smiley Smile' was psychedelic, 'Wild Honey' their (failed) attempt at roots R&B, and 'Friends' is generally regarded as The Beach Boys LP most overtly influenced by TM (Transcendental Meditation). As their career began to decline, every member of the group flirted with TM (ironically, the first convert was Dennis Wilson!), although only Love – and to a lesser extent, Jardine – have remained adherents. While probably not a conscious attempt to hitch a ride on the prevalent "peace-and-love" bandwagon, the outcome was depressingly – and increasingly – familiar: the album was ignored in the US by everyone except diehard fans, resulting in the lowest ever US chart position for an original Beach Boys studio album to date, well outside the Top 100; in Europe, luckily, The Beach Boys were still favoured, and the LP comfortably peaked in the UK Top 20.

Despite the retrospective critical respect accorded 'Friends', it's really not hard to see why it flopped. Although more of a 'real' Beach Boys album than 'Wild Honey' in terms of strong group vocals, and despite its undeniable air of good natured warmth, it has no real direction or focus, a pretty accurate description of the band – and especially Brian Wilson – at the time, as he admitted: "It seems to fit the way I live better... it's simple and I can hear it any time without having to get into some mood. 'Pet Sounds' is by far my very best album. Still, my favorite is 'Friends'".

'Friends' marked an important departure for The Beach Boys in that it was their first official stereo release, the mix being undertaken by Steve Desper who went on to become an integral part of the band's studio set-up, and was instrumental in the creation of two of their classic mid-period albums.

MEANT FOR YOU
(B.Wilson/Love)

A heartfelt invocation by Love sets the tone for the album: short and sweet.

FRIENDS
(B.Wilson/D.Wilson/ C.Wilson/Jardine)

One of the most homespun songs the band has ever recorded – the lyric cannot be anything but autobiographical – this classic waltz (a US Top 50/UK Top 30 hit) is highlighted by harmonica and sterling vocals from Brian and Carl Wilson.

WAKE THE WORLD
(B.Wilson/Jardine)

Buoyed by an amusingly rotund tuba, this track nestles cosily on the overall groove. Brian Wilson and brother Carl handle the lead vocals neatly, while the group chorus (excluding an absent Mike Love) is... just so.

BE HERE IN THE MORNING
(B.Wilson/D.Wilson/ C.Wilson/Love/Jardine)

Another waltz, featuring Brian Wilson singing almost castrato, powerful group harmonies (again minus Love) on the chorus behind Carl and name checks for the Wilson's cousin

(Steve) Korthof, road manager (Jon) Parks – not Van Dyke, as many assumed – and then manager (Nick) Grillo.

WHEN A MAN NEEDS A WOMAN
(B.Wilson/D.Wilson/ C.Wilson/Jardine/Korthof/Parks)

Brian Wilson saunters through the joys of parenthood on this utterly inoffensive number.

PASSING BY
(B.Wilson)

Although lyrics were written to this samba-styled number, Brian Wilson chose to indicate the melody line with a highly effective wordless vocal glide.

ANNA LEE, THE HEALER
(Love/B.Wilson)

Based on a real person, this song's instrumental backing track behind Love's lead vocal harks back to 'Smiley Smile''s simplicity, while boasting superb group vocals.

LITTLE BIRD
(D.Wilson/Kalinich)

Dennis Wilson's first "proper" composition hints at the potential lurking beneath a rough and ready exterior. A surprisingly gentle number benefits from both its composer's plaintive tones (brother Carl also takes a line) and strong group harmonies.

BE STILL
(D.Wilson/Kalinich)

Evocative, even if slightly dirge-like, this Dennis Wilson solo performance was once thought to be a Charles Manson song... not so, but we'll hear more of him later.

BUSY DOIN' NOTHIN'
(B.Wilson)

The very finest of Brian Wilson's "slice of life" numbers (he's the only Beach Boy on the track), his gently understated lead on this essentially solo outing enhances the mood of quiet indolence. The directions, incidentally, are accurate; if you knew where to start, you'd wind up in front of Wilson's Bellagio Road house.

DIAMOND HEAD
(Vescozo/Ritz/Ackley/
B.Wilson)

As session musicians Al Vescozo, Lyle Ritz and Jim Ackley are co-credited on this atmospheric instrumental, it may be reasonable to assume that it developed from a studio jam... but some Wilson watchers contend that this may be recycled 'Smile' material. As ever, proof is lacking, and as with the previous track, the only Beach Boy present is Brian.

TRANSCENDENTAL MEDITATION
(B.Wilson/Love/Jardine)

Generally agreed to be one of the band's lesser musical efforts, this is, considering the subject matter, a strangely dissonant creation. Vocals and backing track often seem to be at odds, and the lyric achieves what many regard as the TM standard (i.e. somewhat uninspired).

WALK ON BY+
(Bacharach/David)

Recorded just after the 'Friends' sessions, this exceedingly brief pass at the Dionne Warwick classic has a vocal tag resembling the legendary Fire Music from 'Smile'.

OLD FOLKS AT HOME/OL' MAN RIVER+
(Foster-
Hammerstein/Kern)

Recorded at the same session as the preceding title, it's presumably Brian Wilson picking his way through the American classic, 'Swanee River', before leading the rest of the band into a song forever associated with the gravel-voiced Paul Robeson. Splendid group vocals are matched by a sprightly backing track driven by a humorous horn arrangement and iced by a cheerful harmonica.

20/20
(CAPITOL SKAO 133 [LP] CDP 7 93697 2 [CD]; RELEASED FEBRUARY 1969)

As the final album under their Capitol Records contract, and given the antipathy between group and label, the fact that '20/20' was less a cohesive project, and more a resting place for sundry odds and ends, spiced with several new tracks, was hardly surprising. What was unexpected was the relative strength of the material, and the emergence of Dennis Wilson both as a composer and a producer... but '20/20' really marked Carl Wilson's assumption of overall creative control of The Beach Boys (a somewhat forced situation as Brian Wilson began his long retreat from recording, composing, The Beach Boys and, ultimately, daily life itself).

'20/20' fared somewhat better than 'Friends' in the US chart – comfortably into the Top 100 – but one fact was incontrovertible: The Beach Boys were still musical lepers in their native land. It would require a change of label and management before the slow climb back to favour could commence. In Britain, as ever, things were quite different: the LP became the group's first non-compilation to reach the Top 3 since 'Pet Sounds', although admittedly its chart life was relatively brief.

DO IT AGAIN
(B.Wilson/Love)

Inspired by a day Mike Love spent surfing, and allegedly based on 'Underwater', a 1961 instrumental by The Frogmen on the Candix label (for whom The Beach Boys also recorded prior to signing with Capitol), 'Do It Again' was rush released just in time to catch the tail end of the summer of 1968 and, slightly surprisingly, just went US Top 20 (the last Beach Boys single to scale such heights for nearly eight years); even more remarkably, it became their second (and last to date) UK Number One single.

An insistent beat backing strong group vocals and a vintage Love lead on a gently nostalgic lyric make this a mid-period classic, produced by Brian and Carl Wilson. This is the only track on the album in mono, and the explanation is bizarre: when compiling the

'Stack-O-Tracks' collection (see below), Capitol managed to lose the master tape. Luckily engineer Steve Desper had made a copy. The building sounds at the fade are part of an otherwise unreleased 'Smile' track, 'I'm In Great Shape'.

I CAN HEAR MUSIC
(Barry/Greenwich/Spector)

Produced by Carl Wilson, and a US Top 30/UK Top 10 hit in early 1969, this cover of The Ronettes classic is felt by many to be the definitive version. Carl's vocal is sweetly robust, and the a cappella break is stunning.

BLUEBIRDS OVER THE MOUNTAIN
(Hickey)

For many years there was a rumour that Ersel Hickey was a pseudonym for Paul McCartney (who was about 16 when Hickey recorded the original). The truth is less glamorous: Bruce Johnston was cutting 'Bluebirds' as a solo single, but willingly surrendered ownership when the band found

themselves short of material for the album. Co-produced by Johnston and Carl Wilson and highlighted by Ed Carter's wailing guitar solo, maybe this was rather too straightforward for the declining fan-following still buying Beach Boys singles in 1968, and it struggled into the lower reaches of the US Top 100 (and the UK Top 40). A significantly more raucous Dutch 45 mix exists, and the 1983 'Rarities' album presented a "split" version.

BE WITH ME
(D.Wilson)

A darkly haunting ballad, heavy with strings and horns, sung and produced by Dennis Wilson. That Charles Manson allegedly had a hand in the writing may account for the ominous air pervading the song...

ALL I WANT TO DO
(D.Wilson)

Manson also reportedly helped Dennis on this flat-out rocker with a less than subtle lyrical message – one for which Mike Love was perfectly suited. The non-musical fade, as you would expect from a Dennis Wilson production, is, according to engineer Desper, precisely what it sounds like.

THE NEAREST FARAWAY PLACE
(Johnston)

An instrumental by turns appealing and saccharine, produced by its writer. Vocals were recorded, but never used (obviously).

COTTON FIELDS
(Ledbetter)

It was Jardine's idea to cover this classic Leadbelly song, and he makes a fair job of the lead vocal. Co-produced with Brian Wilson, this is not the version released as a single (and titled 'Cottonfields' – one word; the latter, a UK Top 10 hit, appeared on LP only on the UK version of 'Sunflower' and is included on both the 'Rarities' CD and the 1993 CD boxed set).

I WENT TO SLEEP
(B.Wilson/C.Wilson)

Sounding like a 'Friends' out-take, this is another Brian Wilson 'lifestyle' item, a gently soporific experience perfectly in keeping with its title. Gossamer group vocals adorn a Brian Wilson production.

TIME TO GET ALONE
(B.Wilson)

This waltz-time song was originally produced by Brian Wilson for Redwood (see 'Wild Honey'), and as re-recorded here by brother Carl, is one of the band's best songs of the late Capitol era. The vocals are uniformly excellent, and the resonant "deep and wide" stuns. A hidden treasure.

NEVER LEARN NOT TO LOVE
(Manson/D.Wilson)

Although not credited as such on any official release, it is now firmly established that Charles Manson's original 'Cease To Exist' was amended only marginally by Dennis

Wilson, resulting in this mildly disturbing yet compelling ode to subjugation. Dennis takes lead vocal as well as producing, and this track was released as the B-side to the 'Bluebirds Over The Mountain' single, thus permitting Manson a fleeting taste of chart glory.

OUR PRAYER
(B.Wilson)

See 'Smile' album.

CABINESSENCE
(B.Wilson/Parks)

See 'Smile' album.

BREAK AWAY+
(B.Wilson/Dunbar)

Released as a single in 1969, 'Break Away' completed the contractual commitment of The Beach Boys to Capitol Records.

A UK Top 10 single and successful everywhere except the US (where it matched 'Bluebirds'), it was another autobiographical Brian Wilson opus. Brian, Carl Wilson, Love and Jardine all take a turn at the lead vocal on a Beach Boys classic that is almost a catalogue of their vocal expertise. Co-writer Reggie Dunbar was in reality Brian's father, Murry.

CELEBRATE THE NEWS+
(D.Wilson/Jakobsen)

A complex song from Dennis Wilson, with excellent use of timpani on the fade, this is thought by many Beach Boys historians to be a comment by the drummer on the end of his relationship with Charles Manson, and was released as the B-side of the 'Break Away' single. Co-author Gregg Jakobsen co-produced and contributed lyrics to Dennis' critically acclaimed 1977 solo album, 'Pacific Ocean Blue'.

WE'RE TOGETHER AGAIN+
(R.Wilson)

Recorded just before the '20/20' sessions, and an excellent example of the group's block harmonies, a melody line from this song later resurfaced in 'Sunflower''s 'Deidre' (see below). The writer is the unrelated Ron Wilson, for whom Brian Wilson produced a single around this time.

Despite the CD booklet credit, copyright documentation makes no mention of Brian Wilson, and additionally there is no evidence that this was the same Ron Wilson who was the drummer of The Surfaris, the California group most famous for 'Wipe Out'.

SUNFLOWER

(BROTHER-REPRISE RS 6382/STATESIDE SSL 8251 (US/UK LP) EPIC ZK 46950 [CD];
RELEASED AUGUST 1970)

Almost universally regarded as the best Beach Boys group album, 'Sunflower' was the product of one of the band's more turbulent periods and emerged only after several line-up changes. That the album was released at all was a minor miracle: drifting without a recording deal after the release of the 'Break Away' 45, The Beach Boys were regarded with extreme circumspection by the music industry, largely due to Brian Wilson's increasingly erratic behaviour, which was perceived as a commercial liability. Their eventual signing to Warner Brothers (and the reactivation of their own Brother Records) was down almost entirely to two people: company president Mo Ostin, with his long standing love of the band, and then-manager Nick Grillo, who convinced Ostin that Brian Wilson would be an active contributor.

Staggering away from the disintegrating Capitol relationship, it initially appeared that the group had walked straight into another war zone at Warners. Their initial submission, 'Add Some Music', was adjudged by the label to be weak, specifically in lacking an obvious single, and was rejected (which Warners apparently were not contractually entitled to do). Manfully, the group set to once more, only for Warners to reject 'Sunflower' (as it was now called) again! At the third attempt, they apparently got it right (or maybe Warners' patience was exhausted) and it was belatedly released.

Catching the band in a rare post-'Smile'

moment of unified creative harmony, 'Sunflower' benefited not only from Brian Wilson's (largely) interested participation as performer, producer and composer, but also from Dennis Wilson's first creative peak and in no small part to the impeccable engineering of Steve Desper, working in the studio he designed at Brian's Bel Air house. Never had a stereo Beach Boys album sounded so good, so crisp and yet so warm... and never had a Beach Boys album sold so badly.

Despite excellent reviews, it charted for only four weeks in the US, peaking just outside the Top 150 (lower than any previous non-compilation), while achieving a Top 30 spot in Britain (albeit briefly). (Note: the original UK LP release included the single version of 'Cottonfields', which did not appear on CD until the Japanese only 'Rarities' release, and was later included on the 1993 'Good Vibrations' CD boxed set, where it was retitled 'Cotton Fields (The Cotton Song)'.)

SLIP ON THROUGH
(D.Wilson)

Dennis Wilson would never be in better voice than on this insistent rocker, a refugee from the original 'Add Some Music' sessions. Inventive vocal lines weave in and out under his lead, whilst Brian Wilson's ethereal falsetto soars. A busy yet never cluttered instrumental track underpins it all. A middling triumph (and an unsuccessful single).

THIS WHOLE WORLD
(B.Wilson)

Clocking in at under two minutes, this is a genuine Brian Wilson masterpiece in miniature, effortlessly coasting through more chord and key changes than you could shake a stick at, with a sureness too long dormant. Brother Carl rises to the challenge with a crystalline vocal, the backup vocals are transcendent in all senses and as before, the engineering is an integral part of the creative process – impeccably clear and detailed. Utterly magnificent, this was also recorded for the 'Add Some Music' album.

ADD SOME MUSIC TO YOUR DAY
(B.Wilson/Knott/Love)

With a lead deftly handed from member to member in a musical relay, and breathtakingly complex backing vocals beaming in from all points of the compass, this soaring ode to the healing power of music is irresistible in its sheer niceness. Another 'Add Some Music' refugee, and a low US Top 100 entry.

GOT TO KNOW THE WOMAN
(D. Wilson)

Teetering on the brink of parody throughout, even super-stud Dennis Wilson eventually breaks up in the midst of a wonderfully over-stated number that nonetheless still enshrines 'Sunflower''s basic tenets of overall excellence in every department. This recording actually dates from the final days at Capitol.

DEIRDRE
(Johnston/B.Wilson)

Developed from a musical theme first used in 'We're Together Again' (from the '20/20' CD, hence Brian Wilson's credit), Bruce Johnston delivers his first fully realised Beach Boys song. Vocals and backing track alike are firmly in the 'Sunflower' mould, yet somehow a slightly clinical air pervades this recording from the close of the Capitol era.

IT'S ABOUT TIME
(D.Wilson/Burchman/Jardine)

One of two tracks newly recorded for the second incarnation of 'Sunflower', this head-down flat-out high octane rocker finds Carl Wilson in sterling vocal form. As with 'Slip On Through', busy, dense even – but never cluttered.

TEARS IN THE MORNING
(Johnston)

Bruce Johnston is in full romantic flow on this slightly saccharine ballad of love lost. An 'Add Some Music' original, it's ably presented, but is still slightly at odds with the overall tenor of the rest of the album. Released as a single, it failed to chart.

ALL I WANNA DO
(B.Wilson/Love)

Another of the late Capitol recordings, featuring outrageous echo married with an inventive tape delay on Love's lead vocal, and Gothic synthesizer slabs and washes, all transforming a simple love song into an almost mystical aural experience, for which Steve Desper deserves major credit. Truly a hidden treasure.

FOREVER
(D.Wilson/Jakobsen)

Quite simply, the most beautiful ballad Dennis Wilson ever concocted... and one of several superb group performances on this album. Brian Wilson's insouciant vocal line at the fade wonderfully expresses the instinctive, almost casual excellence permeating 'Sunflower'. The last of the Capitol-era tracks.

OUR SWEET LOVE
(B.Wilson/C.Wilson/ Jardine)

A thoroughly good-natured amble by Carl and Brian Wilson, wandering here and there, never really going anywhere but enjoying the journey nonetheless. An 'Add Some Music' survivor.

AT MY WINDOW
(Jardine/B.Wilson)

Based loosely by Jardine on the Kingston Trio hit from 1960, 'Raspberries, Strawberries', Johnston supplies the required vocal sweetness to this delicate item, with Brian Wilson contributing the spoken section in somewhat stilted French (rough translation: "A sparrow has arrived and is sitting on my windowsill"). The final 'Add Some Music' hold-over, the closing choral section, was reprised for 'A Day In The Life Of A Tree' on the next album.

COOL, COOL WATER
(B.Wilson/Love)

Brian Wilson's most impressionistic offering so far, highlighted by inventive use of Moog synthesizer (played by Paul Tanner), 'Cool, Cool Water' evolved from 'Smile's 'Love To Say Da Da', the water section of 'The Elements' – and indeed, the strangely evocative water chant uniting the two sections is an original 'Smile' recording. 'Cool, Cool Water' itself was first attempted during the 'Wild Honey' sessions, and part of that recording – released on the 1993 boxed set – may well have been used here; the similarities are striking. Brian Wilson and Mike Love trade the lead over the band's ethereal backdrop. An edited US single release failed to chart.

SURF'S UP

(BROTHER REPRISE RS 6453/STATESIDE SLS 10313 (US/UK LP), EPIC ZK 46951 [CD];
RELEASED AUGUST 1971)

By the time The Beach Boys released their 1971 album, their star was once more in the ascendant, due to a renewed interest in the band from the rock press (most notably *Rolling Stone*, a nice irony considering it was that very magazine which had effectively excommunicated the band almost single-handedly back in 1967), and a string of landmark concerts, beginning at LA's Whisky-A-GoGo and culminating at New York's Carnegie Hall. All that was needed was another album of the quality of 'Sunflower' to cement the return of America's own band...

But, being The Beach Boys, everything in the garden was far from rosy. Dennis Wilson was working on a solo project with Darryl Dragon (aka Captain Keyboards, who soon afterwards achieved stardom with his wife, Toni Tennille, as The Captain & Tennille) and this, coupled with a self-inflicted hand injury which prevented him from drumming for over three years, reduced his contribution to 'Surf's Up' to a minimal level. Brian Wilson, for his part, appeared discouraged by the commercial failure of 'Sunflower' (into which he had invested considerable effort) and preferred to work with his wife and sister-in-law (the resulting album, *Spring* – known in the UK

as *American Spring* – was a homespun masterpiece, full of touches of his wayward genius: needless to say, it died a death despite excellent reviews).

The administrative side of the band was also undergoing upheavals, manager Nick Grillo finding himself increasingly sidelined by newcomer John Frank (Jack) Rieley III, who gradually assumed control over all aspects of The Beach Boys and imposed upon the new album project an uneasy sense of socio-politico-ecological awareness (and whose grandiose journalistic claims were later challenged – no matter, by then he was established). All these changes combined to make

'Surf's Up' an album of far less artistic integrity than 'Sunflower', or for that matter, any of the Capitol releases. In fact, the LP's original title was *Landlocked*... that is, until a Warners employee observed: "If they call the album 'Surf's Up' and include that song, we'll pre-sell 50,000 copies". His name was Van Dyke Parks, and he was absolutely correct. The US Top 30/UK Top 20 album was a critical and commercial success such as The Beach Boys had not seen for many years: but in the long run, the price was probably too high.

DON'T GO NEAR THE WATER
(Jardine/Love)

This opening track neatly outlines the main problems of 'Surf's Up' in general: a slightly hazy production, uneasy lyrics (perhaps forced would be a better word) and an overall sense of trying rather too hard. The sentiment – if not the delivery – is laudable, and the use of Moog was innovative for its time, but the composers apparently found the words on the back of a breakfast cereal carton.

LONG PROMISED ROAD
(C.Wilson/Rieley)

Carl Wilson's first major composition was a quasi-mystical reflection on the trials of life – that is, if Jack Rieley's lyric actually means anything. Lifted by a strident chorus and more Moog textures (mostly contributed by Steve Desper, as on the rest of the album), it fitted perfectly with the tenor of the times, aided by Carl's mellow lead vocal. Twice released as a 45 A-side, it limped into the bottom of the US chart the second time.

TAKE A LOAD OFF YOUR FEET
(Jardine/Winfrey/B.Wilson)

A hold-over from the 'Add Some Music' album, where it was known as 'Walkin'', this manual of pediatric care exudes an aimless charm. Brian Wilson's introductory vocal is taken up by Jardine doing his best Brian Wilson imitation on an oddly amusing song.

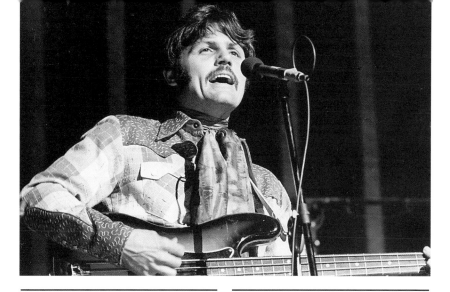

DISNEY GIRLS
(Johnston)

Johnston has often been accused of being schmaltzy if not actually cloying, but here all the elements are finely balanced in a wonderfully evocative remembrance of a simpler, better time that probably never really existed, but should have. Johnston, as ever, is in fine vocal form, and this song was much-covered (by Art Garfunkel, among others)

STUDENT DEMONSTRATION TIME
(Leiber/Stoller/Love)

The band were performing 'Riot In Cell Block #9' (a Fifties favourite by The Coasters) as part of their live show at this time, and Love provided new lyrics to comment on the Kent State University riots of the previous year, when four students were killed by State Troopers sent in by President Nixon. A rau-

cous contrast to the preceding track, featuring police sirens and with Love's lead vocal processed to give a megaphone-like effect, this is undeniably effective, and equally out of step with the rest of the album musically. The new lyric is by turns inspired and forced (sadly rather more of the latter).

FEEL FLOWS
(C.Wilson/Rieley)

A near solo performance by Carl Wilson utilises Rieley's repetitious alliteration to mesmeric effect in a shimmering tapestry of keyboards, guitars, Moog and layered vocals. Jazzman Charles Lloyd provides the flute solo, and Woodrow Theus II contributes the percussion.

LOOKIN' AT TOMORROW (A WELFARE SONG)
(Jardine/Winfrey)

Heavily phased, this sad little tale of itinerant workers is gently understated in a solo performance by its composer. Gary Winfrey's friendship with Alan dates back to pre-Beach Boys days... and strangely, on the original UK issue of 'Surf's Up', his name was omitted from the songwriting credits.

A DAY IN THE LIFE OF A TREE
(B.Wilson/Rieley)

Jack Rieley claimed in a 1982 fanzine interview that Brian Wilson effectively tricked him into singing (?) lead on this stately eulogy to greenery, backed by Wilson himself on pump organ and featuring Van Dyke Parks on the coda. However, this is a strangely compelling track, the very gaucheness of Rieley's vocal enhancing the mood... or is it indeed a classic Brian Wilson put-on, as some suspect ?

'TIL I DIE
(B.Wilson)

Once again, Brian Wilson bares his soul in song to devastating effect, the stark simplicity of the lyric intensifying the mood of resigned melancholy. The group vocal on the verse and especially on the fade is sumptuous. All in all, a strangely gorgeous realisation of despair.

SURF'S UP
(B.Wilson/Parks)

See 'Smile' album.

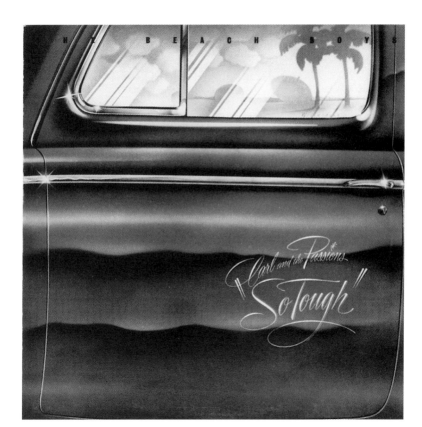

CARL AND THE PASSIONS - SO TOUGH

(BROTHER-REPRISE 2MS 2083 [LP] EPIC ZK 46953 [CD]; RELEASED MAY 1972)

Good fortune and The Beach Boys are seemingly never destined to enjoy any lasting relationship. Following the modest commercial and greater critical success of 'Surf's Up', it all began crumbling (as usual, some cynics might note). A self-inflicted hand injury to Dennis Wilson removed him from the drum stool for the foreseeable future, while the equable Bruce Johnston was having severe doubts not only about Jack Rieley's motives, but also about his honesty, a situation resolved by Johnston's departure – amicably according to him, after a huge blowout with Rieley according to Brian – just before the 'So Tough' sessions. The yawning gaps thus created were swiftly plugged by drafting in the rhythm section from Carl Wilson's protégés, a South African band called Flame. Strangely, no-one batted an eyelid at the quintessential white American band suddenly acquiring two non-white members (nor commented on this early instance of integration) in guitarist/bassist Blondie Chaplin and drummer/keyboard player Ricky Fataar.

A further unbalancing factor was Brian Wilson. If his minimal presence on 'Surf's Up' had been effectively masked by using old vocal tracks, he was all but invisible on 'So Tough', preferring to work with his wife and sister-in-law on the highly regarded collector's item, *Spring*. Hence the scattered compositional credits. 'So Tough' has been called "the four singles album" by more than one noted Beach Boys fan, and it's true - there's the

Brian Wilson/Rieley pair, the Flame single, the Dennis brace and the TM duo, all making for a fragmented album which, whatever the credits may claim, was largely recorded in ten frantic days in late 1971.

In the US, the album came paired with 'Pet Sounds': Warners had acquired the rights to all the Capitol post-*Party* albums and, in a burst of inspired lunacy, decided to issue them in tandem with new material... and according

to the terms of the contract, 'Smile' was part of the deal too! The poor sales of 'So Tough' – propping up the US Top 50 – and unfavourable comparisons universally evoked with the older album, soon lowered the boom on this bright idea (but the band still had to cough up $50,000 in 1973 when 'Smile' failed to appear...). 'So Tough' made the UK chart for a single week.

The production credit for the album reads "Produced by Brian Wilson, Dennis Wilson, Carl Wilson, Mike Love, Alan Jardine, Ricky Fataar, Blondie Chaplin. Especially Carl." Actually, everybody produced their own cuts – Brian excepted – with Carl exercising executive control. This was the first album not wholly engineered by Steve Desper since '20/20'... and it shows. The cover art, however, is outstanding, and the strange title harks back to a high school band name that Brian once threatened his little brother with.

YOU NEED A MESS OF HELP TO STAND ALONE
(B.Wilson/Rieley)

A Brian Wilson composition of some vintage (originally entitled 'Beatrice From Baltimore'), this somewhat ragged, yet insistent, track hints at what the band could have become with greater self-belief. The newcomers are nicely integrated and although the production's rather grungy, in all it's a neat track. For once, Rieley's lyric is both fitting and comprehensible. Carl Wilson supplies a gritty (and poorly double tracked – but it doesn't matter) vocal, and the moving chorus works nicely. The first single from the album, it failed to chart.

HERE SHE COMES
(Fataar/Chaplin)

It might be on a Beach Boys album, but that doesn't make it a Beach Boys track. If you've never heard the *Flame* album, then this is exactly how it sounded – boring, overlong and self-indulgent. Fataar and Chaplin trade the lead, and while other band members presumably appear on the song, you'd never know.

HE COME DOWN
(Jardine/B.Wilson/Love)

One of Mike Love's and Alan Jardine's more successful devotional efforts, exuding a palpable sense of enjoyment from all concerned on a worthwhile track. Mike and Blondie Chaplin take the lead vocals, and the backups, though loose, entice – especially the triumphant "YES I BELIEVE IT !!" (which sounds much better than it looks in print). As for the lyric... well, it's a TM song, OK?

MARCELLA
(B.Wilson/Rieley)

A gem, even if Rieley's words are as near gibberish as makes no difference. Even more than 'Mess Of Help', this shows how the band could have evolved in the Seventies. A rolling track married to some of the best group vocals since 'Pet Sounds' and topped with cracking leads from Carl Wilson and Love – not to mention a wondrous moving harmony tag – make this a middle period classic, shamefully neglected (and, according to Carl Wilson, featuring a vocal contribution from brother Brian). Before Rieley's tinker-

ing, the song concerned Brian's favourite masseuse, and is the final resting place of a melody dating back to 'All Dressed Up for School'. The CD reissue corrected a strange fault during the chorus present in every vinyl version. The second single, which just missed the US Top 100.

HOLD ON, DEAR BROTHER
(Fataar/Chaplin)

More countrified than their previous offering, but equally tedious... and seeming all the worse after such a corker.

MAKE IT GOOD
(D.Wilson/Dragon)

Purloined from the solo project on which Dennis Wilson and Daryl Dragon (pre-Captain & Tennille) were working, this pseudo-Wagnerian soundscape is affecting but also mildly irritating, because it doesn't get anywhere. Dennis emotes tremulously and overdubs himself to great effect on a track that really needs a synthesizer instead of strings. Engineered by Desper, and thus mixed for true quadrophonic sound – an amazing aural experience!

CUDDLE UP
(D. Wilson/Dragon)

Also from Dennis Wilson's solo project, this is a far better realisation of emotion than 'Make It Good', and more of a group effort, whose melody originally belonged to an unreleased DW song, 'Barbara', dedicated to his then wife. Dennis' vocal is as haunting as ever, and Desper's engineering renders a dense track surprisingly uncluttered.

ALL THIS IS THAT
(Jardine/C.Wilson/Love)

Evolving from a track Alan Jardine based around the Robert Frost poem, 'The Road Not Taken', this is the album's quiet highlight, and arguably the best TM-influenced song ever written. Shimmering, hypnotic and beguiling, the vocals from all three composers are gently compelling, the lyric (for once) doesn't jar – in all, probably the best Beach Boys song that Brian Wilson had nothing to do with.

HOLLAND

(BROTHER-REPRISE MS 2118 (LP+EP) EPIC ZK 46952 [CD]; RELEASED JANUARY 1973)

By the summer of 1972, Jack Rieley's influence over The Beach Boys was such that his word was effectively law, and the most obvious result of this state of affairs was the 'Holland' escapade. Ostensibly, the reasoning behind the project was soundly based: during an extensive European tour that summer, the band would relocate en masse to The Netherlands, to concentrate on recording a new album without the distractions Los Angeles afforded.

The reality was far simpler and less businesslike – Rieley was totally enamoured with the Dutch way of life, decided he wanted to live there... and that was that. Preparations for the exodus were as farcical as they were minimal: assuming that the accommodation required could be easily arranged, and that adequate studio time and facilities would be similarly organised, the advance guard were stunned to discover every Dutch studio either booked solid or technically inadequate. Further inquiry revealed a desperate housing shortage, rendering the original plan of basing the band in Amsterdam unworkable. The eventual outcome resulted in The Beach Boys party being scattered up to 30 miles away.

The studio problem was solved in a far more dramatic manner: the band rashly commissioned a custom-built board from engineer Steve Moffit. All he had to do was build it in LA, dismantle it, ship it to Holland and reassemble it in a barn in Baambrugge (staying on to work it...) in less than three months. Not surprisingly, the first test produced nothing but equal amounts of frustration and bad language; the wonder of it was that anything ever worked.

But it did, eventually, by which time a most-unwilling Brian Wilson had also been lured to Holland, a feat achieved by the simple strategy of everyone else (including his entire household) flying on ahead and leaving him

behind in California, bereft of his life support system (even so, it took three attempts to get him on the flight). Once overseas, he continued his indolent lifestyle, and contributed little to the project.

The initial version of 'Holland' submitted was, all things considered, a minor masterpiece. Warners, however, were not so easily impressed. Once again there was no obvious single... and once again Van Dyke Parks held the solution. His intervention led to the weak 'We Got Love' being replaced by 'Sail On, Sailor', and 'Holland' achieved a respectable US Top 40/UK Top 20 position after generally good reviews, and is widely regarded by fans as the best album by the band without much help from Brian. It was also Jack Rieley's nemesis: staying behind in Holland, he intended to manage The Beach Boys at a remove of some 8,000 miles, which provoked a rare act of unity from the band. They sacked him.

SAIL ON, SAILOR
(B.Wilson/Almer/Rieley/ Kennedy/Parks)

As with most perceived Beach Boys history, the saga of the inclusion of this track on 'Holland' is questionable. According to Van Dyke Parks, he sat Brian Wilson down at a piano, told him to write a song and arrived at Warners offices about half an hour later with a cassette copy of 'Sail On, Sailor'... which is true as far as it goes, but Brian had already recorded an early version with Steve Desper engineering back in late 1971 (Desper further contends that the 'Holland' version "sounds awfully like the one I recorded"). Rieley and Tandyn Almer appended new lyrics and the result was the best Brian Wilson/Beach Boys song for many a year, complex lyrically yet musically accessible. Blondie Chaplin's lead is his best work with the band and the harmonies have an invocational quality. Why Ray Kennedy merits a co-composer credit has long been a mystery, although his version with KGB (the 'supergroup' of Kennedy, Barry Goldberg and Mike Bloomfield) allegedly features Brian's original lyrics. As a US single, it charted twice, in 1973 and in 1975, when it just made the Top 50.

STEAMBOAT
(D. Wilson/Rieley)

A suitably chugging track survives some truly impenetrable Rieley lyrics, which Carl handles with grace, if not exactly comprehension.

CALIFORNIA SAGA: BIG SUR
(Love)

Apparently, The Beach Boys needed the perspective afforded by several thousand miles distance to fully appreciate their home state, and this suite expresses that view in three stylistically disparate sections. Love's ode to the mid-California coastline (originally cut during the post-'Sunflower' sessions with a 4/4 tempo as opposed to the waltz-time of this version) works nicely enough as both tribute and travelogue.

CALIFORNIA SAGA: THE BEAKS OF EAGLES
(Jeffers/Jardine/Jardine)

Based on Robinson Jeffers' poem, 'Jeffers' Country', with additions by Lynda Jardine and musical fragments from husband Alan, this section suffers from a malaise common to most spoken word recordings – it doesn't bear repeated listening, especially Jardine and Love's earnestly placid recitation. The musical snatches are frustratingly good, and deserved to become a full song.

CALIFORNIA SAGA: CALIFORNIA
(Jardine)

Introduced by a rare Brian Wilson vocal, this first cousin of 'California Girls' swings along with good humour and energy, Mike Love's excellent lead surfing on a spirited wave of diamond-cut harmonies, and overcoming a slightly self-conscious lyric. The remixed single version (a minor US chart entry, and a UK Top 40 hit) appears on the 'Ten Years Of Harmony' compilation (but not the US CD version – see below).

THE TRADER
(C.Wilson/Rieley)

After his creative hiatus on 'Carl And The Passions', Carl Wilson increases his store of excellent compositions (and productions) with this searing condemnation of the plight of the Native American, then and now. Rieley proves that he can deliver the lyrical goods in the first half before the soft-centred mysticism of the more reflective second section. Carl is in superb voice throughout, and the soaring multi-layered background vocals are awesome.

LEAVING THIS TOWN
(Fataar/C.Wilson/Chaplin/Love)

Even bolstered by classic Beach Boys moving harmony, this is a plodding excuse for a song, superior to the 'Flame' tracks on 'Carl And The Passions' admittedly, but still below the standard required.

ONLY WITH YOU
(D.Wilson/Love)

Carl Wilson's sweetly understated delivery of one of his cousin's better lyrics, and his brother's melody, meanders to considerable emotional effect. Lovely.

FUNKY PRETTY
(B.Wilson/Love/Rieley)

Rumour has it that Brian Wilson is audible during the fade of this diffuse number, but even without him, it's awfully busy, with melodies and vocal lines coming and going without so much as a by-your-leave... and without leaving much impression either. A rotated lead vocal doesn't help any more than the truly lyrically nonsensical middle-eight.

MOUNT VERNON AND FAIRWAY (A FAIRY TALE)

(a) Mt. Vernon And Fairway (theme) (B.Wilson),
(b) I'm The Pied Piper (instrumental) (B.Wilson/C.Wilson),
(c) Better Get Back In Bed (B.Wilson),
(d) Magic Transistor Radio (B.Wilson),
(e) I'm The Pied Piper (B.Wilson/C.Wilson),
(f) Radio King Dom (B.Wilson/Rieley)

Though less than thrilled to be in Holland, Brian Wilson wrote this Fairy Tale, an engagingly eccentric whimsy incorporating childhood recollections and capable of interpretation on several levels. Narrated by Jack Rieley (who claims he had to ad-lib the last 90 seconds) and with Brian supplying the spaced-out Pied Piper voice, as with 'The Beaks Of Eagles', it's the musical fragments which catch the ear. Thankfully the release of the 1993 boxed set saw them presented minus voiceovers and processing, revealing some wonderful musical moments. The rest of the band's reaction to Brian's major submission for 'Holland' was strongly negative, and the eventual decision to include the Fairy Tale as a bonus EP (with a Brian Wilson designed sleeve) was grudging.

THE BEACH BOYS IN CONCERT

(BROTHER-REPRISE 2MS 6468 [LP], EPIC ZK 46954 [CD]; RELEASED NOVEMBER 1973)

As seemed inevitable at this period in The Beach Boys relationship with Warner Brothers, they delivered their fifth album only for it to become their third rejection. 'In Concert' was originally a single disc, and was apparently very nearly rejected again when re-presented as a double album. Ironically, it became the highest charting (US Top 30) and best selling Beach Boys album for Warners to date, doubtless a reflection of their increasingly impressive live reputation (on the strength of this, and in the absence of new studio material, Rolling Stone voted them Band Of The Year in 1974).

'In Concert' is an excellent document of the band's live prowess in the Seventies, and also illustrates just how they integrated the classics with then-new material and a few obscurities such as 'Let The Wind Blow'. Sadly, it wouldn't be long before the oldies

reclaimed centre stage – some of the between song chat hints at the undercurrents already at work in the band.

The line-up for the concerts from which this album was selected included five additional musicians: Carly Munoz (keyboards), Robert Kenyatta (woodwinds), Billy Hinsche (guitar/keyboards), Mike Kowalski (drums/percussion) and Ed Carter (bass).

Full track listing (lead vocalists in brackets): 1. Sail On Sailor (Blondie Chaplin), 2. Sloop John B (Carl Wilson, Mike Love); 3. The Trader (Carl); 4. You Still Believe In Me (Alan Jardine); 5. California Girls (Mike); 6. Darlin' (Carl); 7. Marcella (Carl, Mike); 8. Caroline, No (Carl); 9. Leaving This Town (Blondie); 10. Heroes And Villains (Alan, Carl); 11. Funky Pretty (Carl, Blondie, Alan, Mike); 12. Let The Wind Blow (Carl); 13. Help Me Rhonda (Alan); 14. Surfer Girl (Group, Alan); 15. Wouldn't It Be Nice (Alan, Mike); 16. We Got Love (Ricky Fataar); 17. Don't Worry Baby (Alan, Carl); 18. Surfin' USA (Mike, Alan); 19. Good Vibrations (Carl, Mike); 20. Fun, Fun, Fun (Mike).

WE GOT LOVE
(Chaplin/Fataar/Love)

Wisely removed from 'Holland' to accommodate 'Sail On Sailor', this is another meandering item from the ex-Flame members, further handicapped by dippy devotional lyrics from Mike Love. The band strive to work up a sweat on this live version, but somehow it never really takes off. The studio version – mistakenly pressed up on about 250 German copies of 'Holland' (though not listed on the label) – is truly limp.

15 BIG ONES

(BROTHER-REPRISE MS 2251 [LP] EPIC ZK
46955 [CD]; RELEASED JULY 1976)

The band's failure to sustain the (recording) career momentum generated by 'Holland' and 'In Concert' may seem surprising, but two factors contributed: firstly, Brian Wilson simply didn't want to work with the band anymore, a state of affairs hastened by his declining physical and mental condition... and secondly, the astonishing success of Capitol's 'Endless Summer' compilation (a 1974 US chart-topper which spent years in the charts, and was assembled with such care that the wrong versions of two songs were used) and its UK equivalent, '20 Golden Greats', the first ever Beach Boys LP to top the British chart. These albums not only exposed a new generation of fans to the classic songs (thus creating a new live market) but also sabotaged any creative leanings the band still harboured: bluntly, why struggle to come up with new material in the studio when you can reprise the hits night after night on stage, please the fans and pull in megabucks in the process?

Initially, an equilibrium of sorts existed on the stage, allowing songs like 'Marcella', 'Feel Flows' and 'All This Is That' to sit alongside the hits, but slowly the latter regained prominence, to Carl Wilson's particular frustration; becoming America's premier grossing regularly touring act was scant compensation.

However, there was an unexpected side effect: having heard Brian's songs, everyone wanted to know where he was, and what he was doing. Not much, was the answer. Although still composing, he was a virtual recluse, rarely in the studio, and his mental state was slipping away from sanity. Thus, in a move which seemed sensible at the time, but had far-reaching and ultimately catastrophic consequences, Marilyn Wilson hired Eugene Landy, a therapist with a reputation for getting results with difficult clients via a regime of complete control over their every waking hour. Initially, it seemed to work: Brian began to shed weight and show a renewed interest in recording.

At this point, bells began ringing over in The Beach Boys camp: an attempt to record a new album at Jim Guercio's Caribou Ranch studio in late 1974 had collapsed with only a

handful of songs sketched out... maybe Brian could do the trick, and a new Beach Boys album, produced by – or even just featuring – Brian Wilson, released in America's Bicentennial year, surely couldn't fail.

The album that became '15 Big Ones' (an earlier, ironic, title was 'Group Therapy') underwent several changes in format before release. According to Carl and Dennis Wilson, the original gameplan was for Brian to ease back into production by recording an album of oldies, then one of new material. This was revised to a double album, and then to the single LP eventually released, largely because Brian, after recording over a dozen oldies and a handful of new tunes, announced he'd done enough, and that the album was finished. Recurring reports of studio arguments and emerging divisions within the band may have coloured his decision...

'15 Big Ones' – the title referring to both the band's age and the number of tracks – duly screamed into the US Top 10 (passing 'Endless Summer' on the way)... and descended even faster (again passing the Capitol compilation), also briefly charting in Britain. An album lacking cohesion, the con-trast in production with the 'classic' period was noted, and adjudged wanting, although Brian's extensive use of synthesizer textures was five years ahead of the pack. The "Brian's Back!" promotional hype surrounding the whole project backfired, mostly causing critics to observe that if this was Brian "back", there was still a fair way to go.

ROCK AND ROLL MUSIC
(Berry)

The first single from the album, and the band's first US Top 5 hit since 'Good Vibrations' (but a minor UK Top 40 hit), this energetic cover of the Chuck Berry classic rolls along with high ideals, yet sounds somehow detached: Love's lead vocal is competent, but lifeless. Though the single mix differs in several respects from the LP track, the boxed set version is the LP mix, as the 45 master had deteriorated beyond redemption.

IT'S O.K.
(B.Wilson/Love)

The Sixties revisited! Great backing vocals, a wonderfully 'dumb' bass vocal from Dennis and a throwback lyric triumph over a slightly pedestrian track. Only Mike Love can sing "in the sum-sum-summertime" like that convincingly. Splendid, even if the basic track – featuring Roy Wood and Wizzard on sax – hails from mid-1974. The second single from the album, and a US Top 30 hit – just.

HAD TO PHONE YA
(B.Wilson/Love/Rovelle)

All the band take a line or two of the main vocal – in order, Mike-Alan-Carl-Dennis – but it's Brian's tag that, well, alarms; gruff shading into hoarse, the result of a four-packs-a-day cigarette habit. Aside from that, this is harmless enough, if not original. Brian first recorded a far sparser synth-based version of this in 1973 with Spring (his wife and sister-in-law Diane, the Rovelle in the credits).

CHAPEL OF LOVE
(Spector/Barry/Greenwich)

Brian Wilson's 'new' voice is showcased here in all its roughness, yet it's somehow strangely affecting in this urgent and largely synthesized cover of the Dixie Cups 1964 US chart-topper.

EVERYONE'S IN LOVE WITH YOU
(Love)

Considering he wrote the dippy lyric of this TM-inspired ode, Mike Love seems to be having unusual trouble with the phrasing. A delicate track and backing vocals featuring the Captain & Tennille don't quite overcome the earnestness of intent. Flute trills by Charles Lloyd.

TALK TO ME/TALLAHASSEE LASSIE
(Seneca-Slay/Crewe/Piscariello)

A straight cover of Freddy Cannon's 'Tallahassee Lassie' would have been a far better idea, if the 23 second insert here is anything to go by. Carl Wilson puts some real grit

into the vocal, and the arrangement intrigues. 'Talk To Me', despite Carl's lead, merely crawls along.

THAT SAME SONG
(B.Wilson/Love)

A far simpler production than the rest of the album suits this strange little amble through the history of song. Brian Wilson puts his all into the vocal, and must have really liked the track, as he reused the main riff for the 'Rio Grande' suite on his 1988 solo album.

TM SONG
(B.Wilson)

Recalling the staged studio fights of early albums, the intro to this devotional paean sits uneasily with a bubblegum backing track and kindergarten lyric. Alan Jardine sounds rightly embarrassed.

PALISADES PARK
(Barris)

With a basic track recorded at Western, engineered by Chuck Britz, this is easily one of the highlights of the album. It swings along effortlessly and with a real sense of conviction, not least in Carl Wilson's vocal. Yes, it recalls 'Amusement Parks USA'... that was a good one too. Bizarre that two Freddy Cannon classics should be covered on the same album...

SUSIE CINCINNATI
(Jardine)

Inclusion on '15 Big Ones' was the third outing for this 'Sunflower'-era recording; previously it was the B-side for two singles, 1970's 'Add Some Music To Your Day' and 1974's ultra-rare 'Child Of Winter' Christmas 45 (both were different mixes). An undemanding rocker, with a sassy lead from its composer, the subject of the song was a real cabbie, one Joellyn Lambert... of Cincinnati, of course. The third single from the album, it failed to chart.

A CASUAL LOOK
(Wells)

A noticeably nasal vocal by Love, and a notably excellent one from Jardine can't quite redeem another slightly leaden cover of a 1956 US hit by The Six Teens.

BLUEBERRY HILL
(Lewis/Stock/Rose)

With a restrained intro suddenly exploding into controlled cacophony, and a matching lead from Love, this Fats Domino classic is one of the better covers. Bruce Johnston guests on piano.

BACK HOME
(B.Wilson/Norberg)

Although the song itself dates from 1962, and featured on a rejected early version of 'Sunflower', this was recorded in late 1975 when Brian Wilson visited a Dennis Wilson session. Judging from his lead vocal, Brian had a whale of a time. A literal back-to-my-roots song.

IN THE STILL OF THE NIGHT
(Parris)

Yet another plodding doo-wop cover (of the 1956 Five Satins masterpiece) notable for two vocal contributions – Brian Wilson's still-intact and soaring falsetto, and Dennis' sadly off-key rasp.

JUST ONCE IN MY LIFE
(Goffin/King/Spector)

Brian Wilson's in undeniably ropey vocal form here, contrasting poignantly with brother Carl's effortless glide. The keyboard-based backing track enhances the grainy texture of this cover of the 1965 US Top 10 hit for The Righteous Brothers, making it one of the highlights of the album. To be played at high volume...

BEACH BOYS '69 (THE BEACH BOYS LIVE IN LONDON)

(CAPITOL ST 11584 [LP] CDP 7 93697 2 [CD]; RELEASED NOVEMBER 1976)

Capitol in America, sensing that any Beach Boys product could probably hitch a free ride into the charts on the coat-tails of '15 Big Ones', cast an eye over their back catalogue once more... and discovered a whole live LP, still unreleased in the States. According to Bruce Johnston, it should never have been released anywhere! He claims that when EMI in London babysat the tapes of a live show, someone copied them and, without the band's knowledge or consent, mixed an album out of them, released unsuccessfully in the UK in 1970 as 'Live In London'. The tapes then remained in Capitol's vaults, gathering dust... Contrary to sleeve claims, 'Live In London' was not recorded at the London Palladium, nor at Finsbury Park Astoria (aka The Rainbow in the Seventies) on December 1, 1968 (which was the date of the Palladium gig); the best

guess is the December 8 Finsbury show. Capitol were right: the album reached the US Top 75.

'Live In London' caught the band at a transitional stage in their career, introducing more obscure material among the hits (and a then unreleased out-take, the concert encore of 'All I Want To Do': a studio version of this song appeared on '20/20', and the live version first surfaced on the 1983 'Rarities' album). As their US popularity waned in 1970, they had turned increasingly to foreign markets, especially Europe and in particular England, where they could seemingly do no wrong. 'Live In London' consists of their whole 1968 set (the aforementioned out-take/encore excepted), and the improvement in musicianship from the 1964 live album is impressive (boosted by the addition of a horn section and long serving guitarist "Steady" Eddie Carter)... as is their presentation of complex material ('Wouldn't It Be Nice' and 'Good Vibrations') and vocal prowess; anyone seeking to follow Mike Love's urging to "hear all our mistakes" on 'Their Hearts Were Full Of Spring' will be disappointed. The singing here, as elsewhere on the album, is uniformly faultless... and back

then, Mike really was an ace front man.

All the titles on this album have been covered earlier in this volume. Full track listing with lead vocalists: 1. Darlin' (Carl Wilson), 2. Wouldn't It Be Nice (Alan Jardine, Mike Love), 3. Sloop John B (Carl, Mike), 4. California Girls (Mike), 5. Do It Again (Mike), 6. Wake The World (Carl & Alan), 7. Aren't You Glad (Mike, Alan, Carl), 8. Bluebirds Over The Mountain (Mike), 9. Their Hearts Were Full Of Spring (Group), 10. Good Vibrations (Carl, Mike), 11. God Only Knows (Carl), 12. Barbara Ann (Group).

THE BEACH BOYS LOVE YOU

(BROTHER-REPRISE MSK 2258 [LP] EPIC ZK 46956 [CD]; RELEASED APRIL 1977)

Brian Wilson's distaste for recording was evidently short-lived, for he spent almost all of late 1976 and early 1977 in the studio, essentially cutting solo material with brothers Carl and Dennis occasionally lending a hand. It was also at this time that the services of Landy were dispensed with, his demands and fees alike having become excessive. Several unreleased album titles - some dubious - exist from this period and one, Adult Child, came close to being released in late 1977. However, only 'The Beach Boys Love You' (originally 'Brian Loves You') saw the light of day.

It's an album which polarises opinion among Beach Boys fans and commentators, hence a chart position in the US Top 60/UK Top 30. Some dismiss it for the rough and ready production, Brian's even rougher vocals, and the idiosyncratic song structure and subject matter... others cherish the album for just those reasons, and because it is, title notwithstanding, almost a Brian Wilson solo album. Carrying the synthesized textures of '15 Big Ones' a logical step further, this is arguably Brian Wilson's true comeback album, and a generally satisfying one at that. As a glimpse into his world, it's a fascinating aural document.

LET US GO ON THIS WAY
(B.Wilson/Love)

Carl Wilson does big brother proud on this energetic opener on which Brian plays all instruments (bar the sax – Steve Douglas) and supplies all the backing vocals. Love might have written himself a better middle-eight, but a spanking start to any album.

ROLLER SKATING CHILD
(B.Wilson)

Carl's spare guitar licks aside, it's another solo BW performance, topped off neatly by Love and Jardine on lead vocals, and a gruff

tag from the composer himself. Another gutsy track... and "well oh my/oh gosh/oh gee" may just be the best lyric ever penned.

MONA
(B.Wilson)

Maybe it's the lack of a middle-eight, but, catchy as this cut is, it's not quite up to the standard set by its predecessors. Dennis Wilson's lead vocal struts along nicely, and Brian manages a lyrical tip of the hat to Phil Spector.

JOHNNY CARSON
(B.Wilson)

Answering his own question, "why isn't there a song about Johnny Carson?", Brian Wilson comes up with a truly left-field opus praising the chat show host and US national institution. Love and Carl Wilson's vocals are nicely tongue in cheek, the group backing vocals are solid, and another solo BW instrumental track underpins it all. By now, the listener had either thrown the disc out of the nearest window, or was dancing around the room shouting "yes, yes, more, more!!" It's that kind of track on that kind of album.

GOOD TIME
(B.Wilson/Jardine)

Suddenly Brian Wilson has regained his voice! Well, no... actually this recording dates from the 'Sunflower' era, hence the somewhat lighter production values, horns and solid group vocals (which were much more prominent on the original mix). A 1972 Spring version, also produced by Brian, utilised the original backing track and vocals, adding Moog slabs over the tag. The only 1976 addition is Brian's "hey", on a nice song somewhat out of place here.

HONKIN' DOWN THE HIGHWAY
(B.Wilson)

A glitch in the CD remastering caused the drum intro of the original vinyl version to go AWOL. A medium rocker, maybe not up to the overall album standard but pleasant enough (if unsuccessful as a 45). Jardine's lead vocal replaced Billy Hinsche's original before release.

DING DANG
(B.Wilson/McGuinn)

A late 1973 recording and yes, it's fluff (and yes, it's that McGuinn)... but amusing (once), and above all, short. Love enters the party spirit.

SOLAR SYSTEM
(B.Wilson)

A completely solo performance from Brian Wilson on this recollection of a childhood hobby. Even if the staunchest fans concede a dodgy lyric, the fairground-influenced track disarms... but why no mention of Uranus? Truly a cosmic mystery.

THE NIGHT WAS SO YOUNG
(B.Wilson)

A wonderfully yearning ballad with soaring falsetto from Brian Wilson, heartfelt (if ingenuous) lyric ably handled by Carl over a less dense than usual track, this song reportedly documents one of Brian's more tangled relationships of the late Seventies.

I'LL BET HE'S NICE
(B.Wilson)

There's a tape in circulation of Brian demoing 'Love You' material for the rest of the band, and you can almost hear the jaws dropping when he plays this. A painfully honest letter to a lost love, Brian and Dennis trade gruff verses to great emotional effect, but Carl's middle eight is seamlessly superlative, and the group tag is just icing on the cake. Wonderful stuff.

LET'S PUT OUR HEARTS TOGETHER
(B.Wilson)

Again, Brian comes up with the lyrical goods in this homespun duet with his then wife Marilyn... but double tracking would have helped. Emotion should only be so raw.

I WANNA PICK YOU UP
(B.Wilson)

Brian and Dennis again trade verses on this plodding out-take from the '15 Big Ones' sessions, uniting on the chorus and, amazingly, a neat vocal tag. But still not up to the rest of the album, and thus mildly disappointing.

AIRPLANE
(B.Wilson)

The first section holds out promise, with Love in good, and Brian fair, vocal form, but the rocking tag – apparently stapled on as inspiration waned – undoes much good work.

LOVE IS A WOMAN
(B.Wilson)

A sadly pedestrian closing offering, with only Jardine's "counting" bridge catching the ear. Brian's vocals are very rough, Love's merely facile.

THE M.I.U. ALBUM
(REPRISE MSK 2268 [LP] ZK 46957 [CD];
RELEASED SEPTEMBER 1978)

In April 1977, The Beach Boys – displaying their customary acute business acumen – contrived to sign with a new record label (CBS) while still owing Warners a final album, a situation further complicated in early September by the effective week-long dissolution of the band following a colossal falling-out between Dennis & Carl Wilson on the one hand and Love & Jardine on the other (Brian Wilson remained aloof). The rift was only healed by family ties (however strained) and, some might cynically note, the distinct possibility of losing the CBS advance of a reported $8 million.

The reunion was largely cosmetic and the resolution less than satisfactory, for in the ensuing negotiations, Love had gained control of Brian's corporate vote, thus ensuring that – with Jardine's support – he could always outvote the Wilsons. Eager to fulfil the existing contract as rapidly and economically as possible, the TM axis, pausing only to scoop up a handful of old master tapes, $500,000 worth

of recording equipment and a largely indifferent Brian Wilson, decamped to the Maharishi International University, Fairfield, Iowa, there to attempt a new Christmas album (a rag-bag of mediocre new recordings and old songs dating back to 1970).

To no-one's great surprise (except maybe the TM-ers) Warners turned the album down flat. Forced by circumstance to come up with something, the duo revised some of the Christmas material, polished other rough Iowa tracks and dipped once more into the tape vaults. Brian Wilson was listed as "Executive Producer" above Jardine and touring band member Ron Altbach, the result being a generally listenable, but artistically bankrupt, collection that, in an eerie echo of their first Warners release, exactly equalled the chart statistics of 'Sunflower' – (not too high and not too long).

SHE'S GOT RHYTHM
(B.Wilson/Jardine/Altbah)

Based around a theme written by Altbach for the *Almost Summer* movie (the title track of which was a Wilson/Love/Jardine song of sufficient summeriness to be a US Top 30 single for Celebration, Love's spin-off band), Brian's falsetto lead is perhaps strained, but nonetheless adds a touch of class to an otherwise undistinguished rocker.

COME GO WITH ME
(Quick)

The careless nature of the CBS CD reissue program is graphically illustrated here, with the inclusion of the wrong version of Jardine's near-solo cover of the 1957 Dell-Vikings US Top 5 hit. This is not the original version on the vinyl release of 'M.I.U.', but rather a '15 Big Ones' reject – a boon to collectors, but hardly indicative of a respectful approach to the project. This deplorable lapse aside, this is a notably busier recording than the 'right' one, though by no means objectionable. The correct version – a US Top 20 hit three years later in 1981 – appears on both 'Made In USA' and the 1993 boxed set.

HEY LITTLE TOMBOY
(B.Wilson)

Dating from Brian Wilson's post-'15 Big Ones' period, this sweetened version thankfully omits the original's appallingly sexist middle-eight chatter. Even so, the lyric should concern feminists and parents alike. Love's as smooth as ever, Brian's a mite gruff and Carl sounds like he'd really rather be elsewhere.

KONA COAST
(Jardine/Love)

With Brian's chorus vocal borrowing heavily from 'Hawaii', Love and Jardine trade the lead vocals on this harmless stylistic rehash. A refugee from the Christmas sessions, there entitled 'Mele Kaliki Mako', or 'Kona Christmas': the lyrical differences are minor.

PEGGY SUE
(Allison/Petty/Holly)

This time the wrong – or rather rough – mix as opposed to wrong version of the Buddy Holly classic, this decidedly average cover limped into the US Top 60, doubtless aided by

Jardine's capable vocals. The backing track hails from the '15 Big Ones' sessions, and was set for the Christmas album as 'Christmastime Is Here Again'.

WONTCHA COME OUT TONIGHT?
(B.Wilson/Love)

A smooth Love vocal can't hide the fact that Brian's intro vocal sounds bored and that this mid-tempo ballad is hideously overproduced.

SWEET SUNDAY KINDA LOVE
(B.Wilson/Love)

Neither Carl Wilson's sole lead vocal nor reasonable block harmonies can save this bland ballad from terminal tedium.

BELLES OF PARIS
(B.Wilson/Love/Altbach)

Another Christmas album retread, Love's recitation of the delights of the French capital is both unconvincing and, frankly, insulting.

Quite probably he and Jardine are the only Beach Boys on this track... and it shows. Again, horribly overproduced.

PITTER PATTER
(B.Wilson/Love/Altbach)

Terrific vocals, a restraining hand on the board and not least a halfway decent composition make for the best uptempo track on the album (a relative judgement...). Love and Jardine in good form, and neat pedal steel guitar from Chris Midaugh.

MY DIANE
(B.Wilson)

Another song from Brian Wilson's post-'15 Big Ones' period (from when Dennis Wilson's vocal also dates); even swamped by a totally superfluous string arrangement, Brian's mournful valediction to his then sister-in-law is wonderfully moving. The original, unsweetened version is even better...

MATCHPOINT OF OUR LOVE
(B.Wilson/Love)

A lovely, gentle melody, a mellow Brian Wilson vocal, a nicely understated string arrangement... and some of the most ludicrous lyrics ever to grace (?) a Beach Boys song – a love affair related in tennis terms!

WINDS OF CHANGE
(Altbach/Tuleja)

Once again, not the vinyl version but an incomplete mix of a song that, for all its embarrassingly "cosmic" lyrics, nicely achieves a sense of calm and gentle optimism, due largely to Love and Jardine's mellow vocals. Strings still a mite obtrusive, though... and it would have been nice to have the right mix.

L.A. (LIGHT ALBUM)
(CARIBOU JZ 35752 [LP] 902 127 2 [CD];
RELEASED MARCH 1979)

Seeking to recapture the group spirit so noticeably lacking during the farrago that eventually produced the 'M.I.U. Album', The Beach Boys regrouped in Florida's Criteria studios (owned by The Bee Gees) to record their début for Jimmy Guercio's CBS-affiliated Caribou label. Their contract required Brian Wilson to contribute and produce a specified number of tracks, something it became rapidly evident he was unwilling, or unable, to do. Thus Bruce Johnston received a telephonic summons, ostensibly to lend a hand; he's been with them ever since...

Once again, the archives were raided, this time to better effect. However, the sticking point for many fans and critics was the Johnston-instigated leap onto the then-rampant disco bandwagon with a lengthy remake of an old (1967) Beach Boys song, 'Here Comes The Night' (nothing to do with Them or Van Morrison). Once this was announced,

however good the track might be became irrelevant: the knives were out, and with some justification. The Beach Boys had previously been seen as creators of fads, not followers, thus the album shored up the US Top 100, and at least reached the UK Top 40, unlike its predecessor. As it turned out, the song wasn't too shoddy. The main problem was, it was The Beach Boys. Another problem was an unwieldy, if informative production credit "Produced by The Beach Boys, Bruce Johnston and James William Guercio". Far too many cooks.

GOOD TIMIN'
(B.Wilson/C.Wilson)

Singled out by most reviewers as the disc's standout cut, and the second single from the album, just cracking the US Top 40, the backing track and Carl Wilson's seamless lead vocal date from a series of late 1974 sessions at Jimmy Guercio's Caribou ranch in Colorado. Everything else was added in 1978 to a track often compared favourably to 'Surfer Girl'.

ANGEL COME HOME
(C.Wilson/Cushing-Murray)

Over a sparse and mournful track (recorded in 1976), Dennis Wilson rasps out one of the album's better lyrics with considerable emotional effect.

LADY LYNDA
(Bach/Jardine/Altbach)

Based on Bach's 'Jesu, Joy Of Man's Desiring', and first recorded in 1977, this Jardine production of a tribute to his then wife became a surprise UK Top 10 hit, but bombed in the US. The harpsichord intro is a neat touch, but it's the vocals, both Jardine's lead and the backups, that make this song. Following his divorce, the song was understandably dropped from the live set, reappearing in the Nineties as 'Little Lady'. It also reappeared in 1986 – remixed and partly re-recorded – as 'Lady Liberty', a diabolical B-side tribute to a certain statue's 100th birthday.

LOVE SURROUNDS ME
(D.Wilson/Cushing-Murray)

Extracted from the sessions for his unfinished second solo album, and thus produced by Dennis Wilson, this maudlin dirge expresses exactly his prevailing feelings, something for which his increasingly gruff voice was perfectly suited. The high vocal on the fade is by his then girlfriend Christine McVie of Fleetwood Mac.

FULL SAIL
(C.Wilson/Cushing-Murray)

Carl Wilson almost sleepwalks his way through a soporific number that may not feature any of the rest of the band vocally, bar Bruce Johnston.

SUMAHAMA
(Love)

Lifted from Love's unreleased solo album, 'First Love', and completely re-recorded, this is marginally less offensive than his Parisian travelogue. Presumably inspired by his then girlfriend, Sumako Kelly, who would also have

supplied the Japanese part of the lyric, this song was a surprise UK Top 50 hit single.

HERE COMES THE NIGHT
(B.Wilson/Love)

At 10.52, the longest song The Beach Boys ever recorded... except it's not really The Beach Boys as we know them. Co-producer Curt Becher used his band California to lay down the backing track and the first of many layers of backing vocals, and only Love, Carl Wilson, Jardine and Johnston sing – Brian was hospitalised at the time and Dennis refused to have anything to do with the idea. That said, Carl's lead is nicely gritty, and the moving harmonies halfway through are excellent... but it's all a bit sterile and somehow detached – admirable, but not involving. An edited 45 version managed to reach the US Top 50/UK Top 40 and is available on CD only on a 1995 UK compilation.

BABY BLUE
(D.Wilson/Jakobsen/Lamm)

Another song from Dennis Wilson's "lost"

second album, and one of his very best slow efforts, the textural contrast between his and brother Carl's vocals is striking. Co-written by, and a tribute to his third wife Karen Lamm (formerly married to Chicago's Bobby Lamm), by the time this album was released, she and Dennis were divorced... for the second time.

GOIN' SOUTH
(C.Wilson/CushingMurra)

Cocktail lounge fodder that even Carl Wilson's voice can't redeem. Can this be the same man who gave us 'Feel Flows' and 'The Trader'?

SHORTENIN' BREAD
(Trad. arr B.Wilson)

Brian Wilson originally recorded a spanking version of this with Spring in 1973, but for reasons best known to the band, they chose not to use that backing track. Hence what we have here is an impassioned lead from Carl, a booming bass from Dennis, and a fair degree of fun... but to what end?

KEEPIN' THE SUMMER ALIVE

(CARIBOU JZ 36293 [LP] ZK 36283 [CD];
RELEASED MARCH 1980)

The disappointing performance and reception of 'L.A. (Light Album)', plus heavy pressure from the label, resulted in a swift return to the studio... and to the past. Praying that Brian Wilson might work more effectively in familiar surroundings with people he trusted, the initial sessions for a new album took place in Western studio 3 under the aegis of Chuck Britz, who even resurrected an old valve board.

The success was qualified: Brian apparently remained interested for about three days – and three tracks – before deciding enough was enough, and later in the year, the sessions re-convened at Daryl Dragon's Rumbo Recorders, later moving to the barn – and, weather permitting, the surrounding countryside – at Alan Jardine's ranch up in Big Sur. These later sessions were engineered by Steve Desper.

Once again the archives were raided, and, as with the 'M.I.U.' project, Dennis was absent, dissatisfied with the material and weary of the continuing feud between the Wilsons and the Love/Jardine duo. Bruce Johnston occupied the producer's chair, and the finished product was accordingly workmanlike... and utterly irrelevant to the contemporary marketplace, as, undeniably, were The Beach Boys at this point. An improved US chart position in the Top 75 and a brief UK chart showing hid the fact that it sold far fewer than the 'Light Album'. When they next hit the headlines, it wouldn't be for musical reasons...

KEEPIN' THE SUMMER ALIVE
(C.Wilson/Bachman)

With Randy Bachman, ex-Bachman Turner Overdrive, assisting, Carl Wilson produced a workmanlike retro-rocker to open the album on a promising note. Yes, it veers perilously close to self-parody at times, but a sterling lead vocal by Carl, and some nifty backup vocals – not to mention Joe Walsh on slide guitar – hold out hope for the rest of the set...

OH, DARLIN'
(B.Wilson/Love)

...which evaporates like the morning dew with this turgid ballad, surely one of Brian Wilson's most uninspired, and uninspiring, compositions. Carl tries gamely, as does Love, but the lyric and arrangement suffocate. Brian originally handled the lead vocal, apparently.

SOME OF YOUR LOVE
(B.Wilson/Love)

Things perk up somewhat with this return to High School, first cut at the 'M.I.U.' sessions as 'Mike, Come Back To L.A.', itself based on a chorus riff from 1974's ultra-rare Xmas 45, 'Child Of Winter'. Good block harmonies, a vintage Love vocal and a nifty sax intro overcome a dodgy lyric. Not bad at all.

LIVIN' WITH A HEARTACHE
(C.Wilson/Bachman)

Recorded in the open air, Carl Wilson's lead vocal is the only Beach Boy presence on this undemanding, overlong, pseudo country-rock title, featuring backing vocals from an uncred-

ited Terry Melcher and Curt Becher. The second single from the album, an edited version, failed to bother the charts.

SCHOOL DAYS (RING! RING! GOES THE BELL)
(Berry)

A slightly wonky a cappella intro sets the tone for this formula retread of the Chuck Berry classic, featuring Jardine's enthusiastic vocals, an overbusy mix... and not much else, really. The basic track was cut at the Western sessions.

GOIN' ON
(B.Wilson/Love)

The first single from the album (a minor US hit) showcases a rotated vocal from Mike & Brian, Brian and Carl, a lyric mature if not exceptional, and another plodding backing track, rearranged by Bruce Johnston from Brian's original samba tempo and initially titled 'Tell Me Why'.

SUNSHINE
(B.Wilson/Love)

Based around a version of an old Crystals hit, 'Little Boy', our Boys attempt a reggae style with astonishingly meagre success. All the elements are here, but a complete lack of sympathy with the genre sabotages what were doubtless good intentions. The group vocals try hard.

WHEN GIRLS GET TOGETHER
(B.Wilson/Love)

Very, very slightly remixed, this recording dates back to the 'Sunflower' sessions, from which it was unremarkably cut. Brian Wilson and Love make a good fist of the dual vocals, but the marxiphone-driven track plods tediously along. Why was this preferred to Ed Carter's splendid 'Surfin' Susie'? The answer could well be politics.

SANTA ANA WINDS
(B.Wilson/Jardine)

Considered for the 'L.A.' album and almost

totally re-recorded here – only the first layer of backing vocals and Brian Wilson's harmonica remain, and the lyrics are 100% rewritten – this gentle tribute to what is actually a far from benign meteorological phenomenon transcends some dubious mystical lyrics to paint a cameo of the Southland. Jardine, with Johnston's able assistance and a nasal contribution from Love, emerges with the album's quiet triumph. Note the acoustic bass (presumably by Jardine).

ENDLESS HARMONY
(Johnston)

Heartfelt, if slightly cloying, this tribute to guess who first released as 'Ten Years Harmony', the B-side of a Bruce Johnston-produced California Music 45. A swift rewrite produced a track that, given the events of the ensuing fifteen years, cannot be viewed as anything but hilariously and ironically inaccurate lyrically. Johnston handles the solo first section, Carl Wilson sings about himself in part two. Bizarre.

THE BEACH BOYS

(CARIBOU FZ 39946 [LP] CDCRB 26378 [CD]; RELEASED MAY 1985)

The five years between the release of 'Keepin' The Summer Alive' and 'The Beach Boys' found the band repeatedly in the headlines, usually for all the wrong reasons. Their 20th anniversary in 1981 saw the temporary departure of Carl Wilson, partly to record and promote his eponymous first solo album, but primarily because he'd become utterly disillusioned with the state of the band. To fill the gap, they turned once again to brother Brian, but more often than not his presence and singing were little short of embarrassing, as was graphically illustrated on July 4 during a Long Beach concert televised nationwide – and the rest of the band weren't much better; it was truly a low point in Beach Boys history (although ironically the group returned to the US Top 20/UK Top 50 with 'Beach Boys Medley', one of many such 'Stars On 45'-type hits that year).

Mike Love also released a solo set in 1981, and compared with Carl's lacklustre effort, 'Looking Back With Love' (featuring an uncredited Brian on one track) was – title aside – unexpectedly enjoyable. 1982 was a nothing year for the band, and the beginning of the end for Dennis Wilson: seemingly locked into a downward spiral of alcohol and substance abuse of epic proportions, he was increasingly less able, and willing, to take the stage.

1983 saw three bursts of publicity (and the release of an equally torpid second album from Carl, 'Youngblood'). Firstly, Brian's physical and mental state had declined almost to the point of no return, and Landy was recalled, his immediate removal of Brian to Hawaii leading to "kidnap" headlines; secondly, US Secretary of the Interior James Watt announced a ban on rock bands at the annual July 4 celebrations in Washington, stating that they attracted "undesirable elements", a view seen as an attack on The Beach Boys personally; and thirdly, just after Christmas, Dennis finally pushed his luck once too often and drowned in Marina Del Ray,

past the talking stage) and, at Bruce Johnston's instigation, Steve Levine, then red-hot as Culture Club's producer, was given the job. Sessions began in London in mid-1984, with Jardine and the Wilson brothers helping to lay down backing tracks, before moving to Los Angeles in early 1985 for the vocals to be added. Levine decided that this would be the band's first all digital effort, which removed any sense of immediacy from the proceedings. A further problem was that while Brian was more involved and interested than for many years, the material he brought to the project – as he admitted – wasn't exactly on a par with past glories. The result was a technically perfect yet generally sterile album which tried hard but too often failed to capture either the ear or the heart. It peaked in the Top 60 on both sides of the Atlantic.

swimming while drunk, apparently diving to retrieve possessions lost overboard when his yacht had been moored there.

If any good came of this tragedy, it was that the band reunited to have another crack at recording an album (an attempt with several outside producers in 1982 failed to progress

GETCHA BACK
(Love/Melcher)

An opening drum pattern (programmed, as are almost all drums on the album) that Dennis Wilson would have been proud of leads to a fine opening harmony block, and a typically nasal Love lead... but the real treat on this track is Brian Wilson, with his Billy Joel-esque "whooas", welcome falsetto and a nifty counter vocal on the tag. Nonetheless, and especially on the chorus, the track has a curiously unfinished feel about it. The first single from the album, it went Top 20 in the US.

IT'S GETTIN' LATE
(C.Wilson/Smith-Schilling/Albin-Johnson)

A sumptuous vocal intro (which some claim may be sampled...) and a punchy false chorus with powerful answering vocals – and of course, the standard excellent lead from Carl Wilson – still struggle to overcome a limp verse and chorus melody. The second single, it briefly limped into the US chart.

CRACK AT YOUR LOVE
(B.Wilson/Jardine/Landy)

Brian Wilson plays most of the keyboards on this unobtrusive number, and his middle-eight vocal is nicely plaintive – whereas Jardine's lead seems rather forced – but still, somehow, this mildly urgent track never goes anywhere.

MAYBE I DON'T KNOW
(C.Wilson/Smith-Schilling/Levine/Lindsay)

Gary Moore donates some excellent guitar, and Carl's in good semi-rocking voice, but a repetitive lyric and track can't shake the pervading mood of really not very much of import happening at all.

SHE BELIEVES IN LOVE AGAIN
(Johnston)

Maybe it's the drum programming (by Levine), but the opening track aside, all the songs thus far exhibit a sense of sameness, and this one's no different. Bruce Johnston and Carl Wilson share the vocal duties, with the former sounding (unusually) less than silky smooth.

The third single, which failed to chart.

CALIFORNIA CALLING
(Jardine/B.Wilson)

Real drums this time (played by one R. Starkey) up the energy level several notches and make this surfin' song for the Eighties an album highlight. Love and Jardine sound as if they're having fun, the backups convince, Brian Wilson hollers effectively... and why this wasn't a single is an eternal mystery.

PASSING FRIEND
(O'Dowd/Hay)

Carl Wilson tries his utmost, but this second-string Culture Club discard really isn't appropriate, nor up to par. It's also way too long.

I'M SO LONELY
(B.Wilson/Landy)

Try as he might, Steve Levine can't disguise that this is one of Brian Wilson's more simplistic, though in no way objectionable, compositions. The move to a slightly higher register may not have been such a good idea for Brian,

though Carl handles the middle-eight with his usual aplomb.

WHERE I BELONG
(C.Wilson/White-Johnson)

Proof that Carl Wilson can still come up with the compositional – as well as the vocal – goods, this is simply magnificent, with block harmonies of almost chilling power and a superb vocal counter from Jardine on the chorus. Give the Boys some good material and watch 'em go to it! The undoubted album highlight.

I DO LOVE YOU
(Wonder)

Not content with merely writing this track, Stevie Wonder also weighs in with drums, bass, keyboards and harmonica... but still, the overall effect is of Carl Wilson singing on someone else's album. It's good – but it's not The Beach Boys.

IT'S JUST A MATTER OF TIME
(B.Wilson/Landy)

A concert staple throughout 1983, Brian Wilson's affection for The Four Freshmen is evident on this meandering, if amiable, original. He and Love share the vocals while the rest of the band back more than adequately.

MALE EGO
(B.Wilson/Love/Landy)

The most Brian Wilson-like track on the album (although not a BW production, however much it may sound like it), with his urgent vocal moving things along at a smart clip. The lyric, alas, gives severe pause for thought, on a par with the legendarily sexist 'Hey Little Tomboy'. Whatever, given a choice, many fans would prefer this Brian-ish style of production.

STILL CRUISIN'
(CAPITOL C1 92639 [LP] CDP 7 92639 2 [CD];
RELEASED AUGUST 1989)

Another four years down the line, and by the time of this 'new' album, two astonishing events have occurred: Brian Wilson has effectively left the band, releasing a critically acclaimed solo album, 'Brian Wilson' (1988, a US Top 60 entry), and also in 1988, The Beach Boys released a million-selling #1 hit, over twenty years since their last, 'Good Vibrations'. 'Kokomo', taken from the soundtrack of the Tom Cruise movie Cocktail, hung around for a few months before commencing an inexorable journey up the charts. This was enough to secure a one-off album deal with the old enemy, Capitol, and the concept was expanded to include other Beach Boys titles featured in movies, plus three new songs and another surprise chart hit, a duet with rap trio The Fat Boys.

Almost certainly on the strength of the inclusion of 'Kokomo', this strange hybrid went US Top 50 and eventually sold over 700,000 copies, giving the band their first gold

album since '15 Big Ones'. Even so, 'Still Cruisin'' sounds about as cohesive as you'd imagine... Unless stated, all tracks are produced by Terry Melcher. (Three Sixties classics, 'I Get Around', 'California Girls' and 'Wouldn't It Be Nice', are dealt with earlier in this volume.)

STILL CRUISIN'
(Melcher/Love)

Hailing from the *Lethal Weapon 2* movie, this musical son of 'Kokomo' slopes along amiably enough, with a lead vocal each for Love, Johnston, Carl Wilson and Jardine and some perennially dodgy Love lyrics. As a single, it only just charted in the US in the lowest ever position achieved by The Beach Boys.

SOMEWHERE NEAR JAPAN
(Phillips/Melcher/Love/Johnston)

Widely regarded by Beach Boys fans as the last halfway decent song they've released to date, the mildly confusing lyric begins to make sense with the knowledge that the Phillips is Papa John, and that it recounts his daughter's

less than romantic honeymoon experience on the island of Guam. The block harmonies in the verses are snorters, and Love, Carl and especially Jardine – the latter forsaking accuracy for effect – turn in some sterling vocal work. Reportedly, when informed of the many drug references in the lyrics, Jardine refused to sing it live! Released – in a remix – as the second single from the album, it failed to chart.

ISLAND GIRL
(Jardine)

Based very, very loosely on the Dell-Vikings classic, 'Whispering Bells', this second reggae attempt fares better than 1980's 'Sunshine'. Once again, Love, Carl and Jardine share the lead vocal, and yes, that is Brian Wilson on the intro – added some time after the track was completed in the interests of "unity". The credits state "A Red Barn production"... meaning Jardine, presumably.

IN MY CAR
(B.Wilson/Landy/Morgan)

A late inclusion, this percussion-based Wilson opus has its moments, although the lyric isn't among them. A slightly frenetic effort, Brian's vocals were augmented by Carl Wilson and Alan Jardine to make it appear less of a solo track – which is, of course, exactly what it was. Produced by Brian Wilson and, allegedly, Dr.Eugene Landy.

KOKOMO
(Phillips/Love/Melcher/McKenzie)

The majority of this composition dates back to 1984, when Phillips and McKenzie (for whom Phillips had written and produced 'San Francisco' back in 1967) spent a few days at Virginia Beach, so one really can't blame Love and Melcher too much. Absolute soundtrack fodder and somewhat less convincing than 'Island Girl', it can't be denied that the chorus moves along nicely... nor that over a million Americans purchased a copy. Isn't life strange? A UK Top 30 hit, the Boys – including Brian this time – later re-recorded the lyric in Spanish.

WIPE OUT (WITH THE FAT BOYS)
(The Surfaris)

There's a great story in here somewhere... Originally, The Beach Boys were due to record this with Run DMC, but Love – allegedly – cut his own deal on the side, hence the collaboration we have here, an unexpected Stateside Top 20 entry (and nearly a UK chart topper !). Actually, it's a whole mess of fun (unless you're a surf purist) and live takes on a new dimension, with longtime sideman Billy Hinsche taking over The Fat Boys part(s). Produced by The Latin Rascals in association with The Beach Boys... and here's a strange thing. At least one noted Beach Boys historian maintains that the only BB vocals heard on this track belong to Brian Wilson. The truth is out there...

MAKE IT BIG
(Melcher/House/Love)

From the film *Troop Beverly Hills* (although the movie version is a different mix), Carl, Love and Jardine's vocals lift this anonymous song into the acceptable range – just. Brian Wilson pops up on the tag.

SUMMER IN PARADISE

(BROTHER ENTERTAINMENT R 727-2 [CD
ONLY]; RELEASED AUGUST 1992. EMI CDEMD
0777 7 81036 2 2; UK REVISED VERSION –
RELEASED JUNE 1993)

The absolute nadir of their recording career, 'Summer In Paradise' answers an oft-posed question – what would a Beach Boys album with absolutely no active Brian Wilson involvement sound like? Pointless, vapid and soulless is the reply. The performances and production (by Terry Melcher) are faultless, the material utterly disposable. And it could have been worse, for during the early stages of recording, Alan Jardine was "suspended" from the band, reportedly due to a severe attitude problem, reinstatement coming only during the final weeks of the project.

Given a universal thumbs down by critics and fans alike, the sales were disastrous (according to a source close to the band, less than 1,000, according to one of the Boys 145,000 – this latter figure probably represents the number shipped to the shops and it became the first ever original Beach Boys

album not to chart: so the band decided to remix and partly re-record five tracks, thus tossing good money after bad. After all that, this revised version was only ever released in Europe. In mitigation, it must be admitted that the packaging of the original US issue was outstanding: shame about the music.

HOT FUN IN THE SUMMERTIME
(Stone)

The first 'single' from the album was this workmanlike if slightly brittle cover of the old Sly & The Family Stone hit. Carl Wilson and Mike Love's vocals are spot on, but even this early on in the proceedings, a feeling of "doing it by numbers" is evident.

SURFIN'
(B.Wilson/Love)

One of the set's (relative) successes, this reworking of The Beach Boys first ever single in a Nineties style is at least interesting. Just as 31 years earlier, Love handles the lead vocal, with solid support from Carl.

SUMMER OF LOVE
(Love/Melcher)

Quite possibly the worst set of lyrics that Mike Love has ever concocted marry with a tepid track for a song that was originally intended to be a collaboration with Bart Simpson! Love does his best vocally, and this track, perhaps appropriately, turned up in a 1995 episode of *Baywatch*.

ISLAND FEVER
(Melcher/Love)

Repetitive track, dopey lyric, reasonable vocals from Love and Carl... you begin to get the idea. When the band radically reworked the song, they actually made a bad track even worse.

STILL SURFIN'
(Love/Melcher)

Actually, this isn't too bad compared with the rest of the album, with great harmonies on the chorus just about offsetting a misguidedly ecological lyric. Love's in good form, plus some nifty drums (probably electronic).

SLOW SUMMER DANCING (ONE SUMMER NIGHT)
(Johnston/Webb)

The classic 'One Summer Night' severely shows up Bruce Johnston's new 'Dancing' section, just as Jardine outshines him vocally. There are far better slow songs.

STRANGE THINGS HAPPEN
(Melcher/Love)

Another small triumph for Jardine on the chorus of this mid-tempo number, while Mike Love struggles with his own dire mystical lyric. The revised version had well over a minute of the overlong fade excised. Words aside, not too bad.

REMEMBER "WALKING IN THE SAND"
(Morton)

One of the worst cover versions of anything, by anybody, anywhere, at any time. There is absolutely nothing about this track to commend.

LAHINA ALOHA
(Melcher/Love)

Once again, good group chorus vocals come to the rescue of mediocrity. Once again, Carl Wilson and Love in good voice. Once again, a sense of detachment. Accordion by Van Dyke Parks, by the way.

UNDER THE BOARDWALK
(Resnick/Young/Love)

It's difficult to go too far wrong with this classic, but Love tries anyway by adding new words. A slow, gentle rendering, with sweet leads from Carl and Love, the revised version wisely restores the full bridge, ably handled by Jardine.

SUMMER IN PARADISE
(Love/Melcher/Fall)

Up to the point where Love mentions "an ozone layer", this is very reasonable – all 40 seconds of it. Thereafter, despite a backing track and harmonies well above the album average, the appallingly trite lyrics sabotage what could have been a nice little song... not a classic by any means, but a reasonable second-division number. The revised version is even worse, by virtue of Roger McGuinn adding not only a very shaky vocal but also lashings of jangly guitar.

FOREVER
(D.Wilson/Jakobsen)

A sympathetic vocal from US sitcom heart-throb (and occasional Beach Boys tour drummer) John Stamos, and some sweet accordion from Van Dyke Parks, help ease the somewhat hard edge grafted uneasily onto Dennis Wilson's gorgeous ballad. Unlike the rest of the songs, at least Stamos shows respect for the material. Produced by Stamos, Gary Griffin & Lanny Cordola, the revised version features a subtle remix.

STARS AND STRIPES

(RELEASED AUGUST 1996)

Whether this is genuinely a Beach Boys album is a matter for conjecture, as the group members are featured as backing vocalists on this collection of country-styled cover versions of mostly well known (over familiar?) songs from around thirty years ago. The general consensus among Beach Boys admirers is that overall it wasn't the best idea the group have ever had. Co-produced by Brian Wilson (who supervised the vocals) and Joe Thomas (who oversaw the rest of it), the group (plus Matt Jardine, Alan Jardine's son, by now a semi-official member) vocally support such country music luminaries as Willie Nelson, Timothy B. Schmit (of the latter day Eagles) and ten others on cover versions of very variable quality. Nelson and Schmit (the latter with a Jimmy Webb string arrangement) are regarded as by far the best, while the lowest points accrue to 'I Get Around', 'Be True To Your School' and 'Sloop John B'. The point of this exercise seemingly avoided any considerations other than those of accountants and marketing executives – no one asked why (which also applied to the 1996 collaboration between Status Quo and The Beach Boys, which also produced a cover version of 'Fun Fun Fun'). Apparently, there's even a second volume planned – we can hardly wait.

Track listing (lead vocalist in brackets): 1. 'Don't Worry Baby' (Lorrie Morgan), 2. 'Little Deuce Coupe' (James House), 3. '409' (Junior Brown), 4. 'Long Tall Texan' (Doug Supernaw), 5. 'I Get Around' (Sawyer Brown), 6. 'Be True To Your School' (Toby Keith), 7. 'Fun Fun Fun' (Ricky Van Shelton), 8. 'Help Me Rhonda' (T. Graham Brown), 9. 'The Warmth Of The Sun' (Willie Nelson), 10. 'Sloop John B' (Collin Raye), 11. 'I Can Hear Music' (Kathy Troccoli), 12. 'Caroline, No' (Timothy B. Schmit).

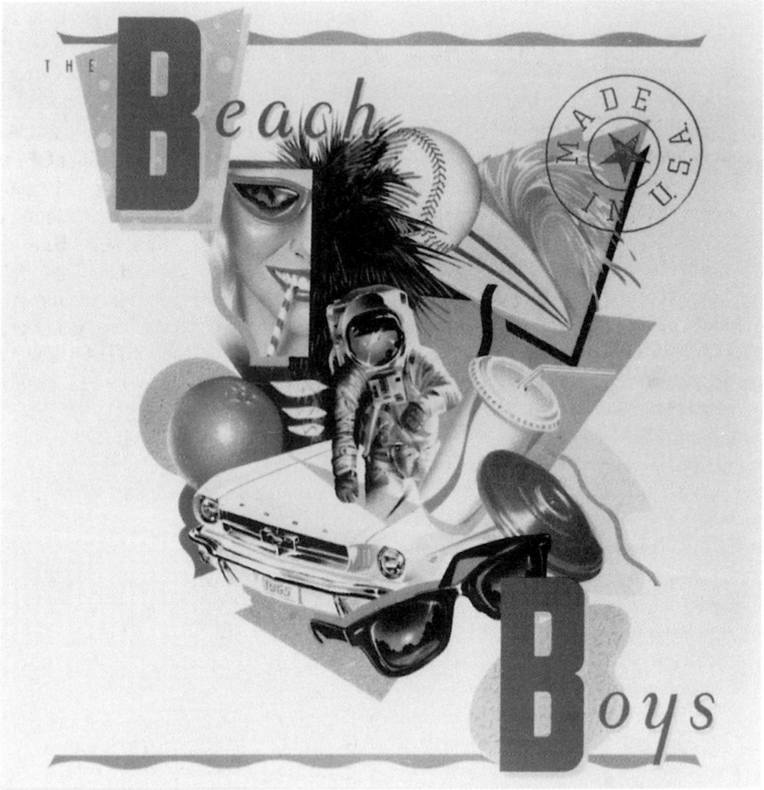
THE
Beach
MADE IN U.S.A.
1965
Boys

COMPILATIONS

With the probable exception of Elvis Presley, The Beach Boys are unquestionably the most repackaged act of the rock era. Beginning in 1966 with Capitol's 'Best Of The Beach Boys', there are now innumerable compilations world-wide, ranging from the sublime to the bizarre (notably Japan's 'Instrumental Hits' collection...). Most are little more than variations on the well-worn greatest hits/classics theme – and thus won't be dealt with here apart from a couple of recommendations below – but there is a clutch which, in addition to presenting a well-considered track listing, features material otherwise unavailable or previously unreleased. In the albums considered below, only those tracks not previously dealt with will be discussed. The very best compilation of all (and probably ever) is the Capitol 5CD boxed set, 'Good Vibrations - 30 Years Of The Beach Boys', covered at the end of this chapter.

For those who regard the Boxed Set as somewhat too comprehensive for their requirements, the classic years are ably covered by '20 Golden Greats' (Capitol EMTV 1), with all the important hits, which topped the UK charts for ten weeks in 1976, while 1990's 2 CD set 'Summer Dreams' (Capitol EMTVD 51), casts a somewhat wider net.

STACK-O-TRACKS
(Capitol DKAO 2893 [LP]
CDP 7 93698 2 [CD];
released August 1968)

Well in the running for the "strangest compilation ever released" title, this instant collector's item comprised just the instrumental tracks of fifteen of the band's greatest hits and best-known classics. Reportedly selected by Carl personally, the removal of the vocals allowed the complexity and beauty of Brian Wilson's compositions to shine through. Better yet was the CD reissue, for not only were there three

additional tracks, but also several cuts previously in mono turned up in glorious stereo. Not Brian's stereo, granted... but it's still great to hear.

Full track listing (with stereo tracks noted #, bonus cuts noted *): 'Darlin''/'Salt Lake City'#/'Sloop John B'#/'In My Room'/'Catch A Wave'/'Wild Honey'/'Little Saint Nick'/'Do It Again'/'Wouldn't It Be Nice'#/'God Only Knows'#/'Surfer Girl'/'Little Honda'#/'Here Today'#/'You're So Good To Me'#/'Let Him Run Wild'#/'Help Me, Rhonda'*/'California Girls'*#/'Our Car Club'*.

TEN YEARS OF HARMONY
(Epic 37445 [LP] 2 ZK
37445 [CD]; released
November 1981)

A woefully inaccurate title aside, this survey of the Warners and Caribou eras boasts a thoughtful track selection, sundry alternate versions and two previously unreleased songs, both featuring Dennis. However, on the American CD release (but not the European!), some of the alternates were replaced by the standard versions (noted*).

Full track listing: 'Add Some Music To Your Day'/'Roller Skating Child'/'Disney Girls'/'It's A Beautiful Day' (45 edit)/'California Saga-California' (45 mix)*/'Wontcha Come OutTonight'/'Marcella'/'Rock And Roll Music' (45 mix)*/'Goin' On'/'It's O.K.'/'Cool, Cool Water' (45 edit)/'San Miguel' (unreleased)/'School Day' (unreleased 45 mix)*/'Good Timin''/'Sail On, Sailor'/'Darlin'' (live)/'Lady Lynda' (LP version)/'Sea Cruise' (unreleased)/'The Trader'/'This Whole World'/'Don't Go Near The Water'/'Surf's Up'/'Come Go With Me'/'Deirdre'/'She's Got Rhythm'/'River Song' (Dennis solo)/'Long Promised Road'/'Feel Flows'/'Til I Die'

IT'S A BEAUTIFUL DAY
(Jardine/Love)

Composed for the 1979 *Americathon* movie, this amiable mid-tempo rocker is better than most of that year's 'L.A. (Light Album)'. Produced by Johnston (and with no involvement from Brian), Carl, Love and Jardine tackle the vocals with some verve, and the track is nicely restrained. The single missed the charts.

SAN MIGUEL
(D.Wilson/Jakobsen)

Dating from 1969, and the transitional Capitol/Warners period, this Dennis-produced rocker showcases fine vocals from Carl, energetic fuzz guitar from Eddie Carter, horns, castanets, the works.

SEA CRUISE
(Smith)

Dennis struts along nicely on this recycled Frankie Ford Fifties evergreen. Brian seems to be the only other Beach Boy present vocally, and overall, the track (a '15 Big Ones' reject produced by Brian), exhibits an unfinished air. Still fun, though.

The full LP track listing (with then-unreleased tracks noted*) was: 'With A Little Help From My Friends'*/'The Letter'*/'I Was Made To Love Her'/'You're Welcome'/'The Lord's Prayer'/'Bluebirds Over The Mountain' ('split' Dutch mix)/'Celebrate The News'/'Good Vibrations'/'Land Ahoy'*/'In My Room' (German lyric)/'Cotton Fields'/'All I Want To Do' (live)/'Auld Lang Syne'.

BEACH BOYS RARITIES
(CAPITOL ST-12293 [LP] TOSHIBA-EMI TOCP 6604 [CD]; RELEASED SEPTEMBER 1983)

Exactly why Capitol decided to put out this collector's item – in both senses of the word – isn't clear. It's an odd patchwork of alternates, B-sides and unreleased tracks, and was swiftly withdrawn under threat of legal action by The Beach Boys (no idle threat, either!) who considered the album substandard. The words "pot", "kettle" and "black" spring to mind... 'Rarities' has only been issued on CD in Japan, with the addition of three 'bonus' medleys. The full LP track listing (with then-unreleased tracks noted*) was: 'With A Little Help From My Friends'*/'The Letter'*/'I Was Made To Love Her'/'You're Welcome'/'The Lord's Prayer'/'Bluebirds Over The Mountain' ('split' Dutch mix)/'Celebrate The News'/'Good Vibrations'/'Land Ahoy'*/'In My Room' (German lyric)/'Cotton Fields'/'All I Want To Do' (live)/'Auld Lang Syne'.

WITH A LITTLE HELP FROM MY FRIENDS
(Lennon/McCartney)

Cut during the 'Wild Honey' sessions, "just to see how we would sound", according to lead vocalist Johnston. The answer would seem to be, "stoned"... but in fact, there's a perfectly good explanation. Apparently, while recording the backing vocals, rather than sing high, the band slowed the track down (an old trick)... only no-one told the mastering engineer in 1983.

THE LETTER
(Carson)

This version of The Box Tops hit was recorded during rehearsals in Los Angeles for a 1967 Hawaii concert, hence the sparse instrumentation. Whether the vocal is by Brian or Carl is still open to debate.

COTTON FIELDS
(Ledbetter)

It was a sign of either The Beach Boys' increasing confidence in their own judge-

ment – or of Brian Wilson's diminishing influence – that Jardine decided the version of this song he'd produced with Brian for '20/20' could be improved. The last Beach Boys song ever issued only in a mono format and notable for its beefed-up backing vocals and steel guitar (provided by O.J. "Red" Rhodes), Jardine's revision charted high in just about every market... except the USA, where it missed completely.

MADE IN USA

(CAPITOL STBK - 12396 [LP] CDP 46324 [CD];
RELEASED AUGUST 1986)

Commemorating The Beach Boys' 25th anniversary, Capitol not only assembled this well considered retrospective (understandably heavy on the 62-66 period) but also offered two new tracks. The only glitch was some dodgy remastering which did terrible things to Love's vocal on 'Wouldn't It Be Nice. Full track listing; 'Surfin' Safari'/'409'/'Surfin' USA'/'Be True To Your School' (45 version)/'Surfer Girl'/'Dance, Dance, Dance'/'Fun, Fun, Fun'/'I Get Around'/'Help Me, Rhonda' (45 version)/'Don't Worry, Baby'/'California Girls'/'When I Grow Up...'/'Barbara Ann' (45 edit)/'Good Vibrations'/'Heroes And Villains'/'Wouldn't It Be Nice'/'Sloop John B'/'God Only Knows'/'Caroline, No'/'Do It Again' (45 version)/'Rock And Roll Music' (LP mix)/'Come Go With Me'/'Getcha Back'/'Rock And Roll To The Rescue'/'California Dreamin''.

ROCK AND ROLL TO THE RESCUE
(Love/Melcher)

Produced by Terry Melcher (and during the initial sessions, an uncredited Brian), this semi-autobiographical rocker clatters along at high speed, with tongue firmly planted in cheek and Brian in fine fettle, with Carl and Jardine not far behind. A US Top 75 hit.

CALIFORNIA DREAMIN'
(Phillips)

Slightly bettering 'Rescue' as a single, this energetic cover of the Mamas And Papas classic is actually a revised version – overseen by Melcher – of his 1983 production for The Beach Boys, which only ever saw the light of day on a compilation cassette available from the Radio Shack chain of stores in the US. The basic changes are the dropping of Love's vocals, the addition of Roger McGuinn's jangly guitar and a more upfront drum track. Jardine and Carl are in sterling form.

LOST AND FOUND (1961-62)
(DCC DZS-054; RELEASED FEBRUARY 1991)

Tracking down the original session tapes allowed DCC to present the entire Beach Boys pre-Capitol recordings in superb quality, not to mention unimproved (?) by Murry! Although, to be frank, these tracks are of little musical merit, the historical context is of immeasurable importance, indicating that Brian's desire to control studio matters began very early indeed. Of the 21 tracks on the CD, 5 are of studio chat. The full listing (of songs only, the master takes noted *) is: 'Luau(demo)'/'Surfin''(demo)'Surfin''/ 'Surfin''*'/'Luau'/'Luau'*'/'Barbie'/ 'What Is A Young Girl Made Of?'/'Surfin' Safari'/'Surfin Safari'*'/'Judy'/'Judy'*'/'Beach Boys Stomp'/'Surfin Safari'' (overdub attempt)/'Lavender' (demo).

LUAU
(B.Wilson)

Recorded, with the 'Surfin'' and 'Lavender' demos, in Hite Morgan's home studio, all these titles indicate that a fair degree of practising has been going on. Carl's guitar is the sole accompaniment. Unlike 'Surfin'', 'Luau' doesn't really convince lyrically. Dennis and Brian take the leads. Strangely, the studio takes are less enjoyable than the demo version...

SURFIN'
(B.Wilson/Love)

The demo version lacks the intro (it obviously hadn't been worked out yet) but the rest of the song's looking good. Taken at a slightly fast clip.

BARBIE
(B.Morgan)

Released as by Kenny and The Cadets, and heard here in stereo for the first time, this is actually Brian backed up by Jardine, Carl and mom, Audree. The Morgan's son Bruce penned this piece of standard teen slop.

WHAT IS A YOUNG GIRL MADE OF?
(B.Morgan)

Brian solo this time, with a positively alarming falsetto. The B-side of the previous track, and also a stereo début.

SURFIN' SAFARI
(B.Wilson/Love)

Notably lyrically different, the earlier of the two takes was somehow released as a 45 in West Germany! A later attempt at overdubbing proved disastrous.

SURFER GIRL
(B.Wilson)

Even in this primitive form, a beautiful song shines through.

JUDY
(B.Wilson)

A cheerfully upbeat number, the Judy in question was Brian's then girlfriend.

BEACH BOY STOMP
(C.Wilson)

Also known as 'Karate', this game essay at a surf instrumental marks the composing début of the youngest Wilson (and also provided the name for the long-running UK fan magazine).

LAVENDER
(D.Morgan)

Written by Hite Morgan's wife, Dorinda, the natural blend of the Boys' voices is illustrated by this Four Freshmen-derived number. A helping hand from Brian is suspected in the arrangement.

GOOD VIBRATIONS - THIRTY YEARS OF THE BEACH BOYS

(CAPITOL C2 7 81294 2 [CD ONLY]; RELEASED NOVEMBER 1993)

Having acquired the rights to the entire Beach Boys back catalogue, Capitol set about following their highly successful, and critically acclaimed, Twofer reissue program with something even more ambitious – a complete career retrospective. Boasting considerable input from collectors and Beach Boys historians world-wide, the result was that rare beast, a compilation accessible to the general public that was also a delight for the hard-core fan. The credit for this goes to the triumvirate charged with producing the compilation, **David Leaf** (Brian Wilson biographer and author of the Twofer booklets), **Andy Paley** (Brian's collaborator and right-hand man of many years standing) and **Mark Linnet** (Brian's engineer since the late 1980s).

The vaults were ransacked to impressive effect, the jewel of the set being some 30 min-utes of 'Smile' material previously available only on bootlegs; further wonders were to be found in a fifth CD composed entirely of collector's items such as sessions for 'Pet Sounds' songs, previously unheard live material, and even more 'Smile' tracks. Presented with a superb 60-page booklet written by David Leaf, and making a point of repeating as few bonus tracks from the Twofers as possible, the set was universally praised, and contributed considerably to some revisionist thinking in the ongoing Beach Boys *vs.* Beatles debate.

Full track listing (tracks noted # are previously unreleased, or an alternate version; those noted * are live tracks):

CD 1 – 'Surfin' USA' (demo)#/'Little Surfer Girl'#/'Surfin'' (rehearsal)#/'Their Hearts Were Full Of Spring'#/'Surfin' Safari'/'409'/'Punchline'#/'Surfin' USA'/'Shut Down'/'Surfer Girl'/'Little Deuce Coupe'/'In My Room'/'Catch A Wave'/'The Surfer Moon'/'Be True To Your School' (45 version)/'Spirit Of America'/'Little Saint Nick' (45 mix)/'Things We Did Last Summer'#/'Fun, Fun, Fun'/'Don't Worry, Baby'/'Why Do Fools Fall In Love?'/'The Warmth Of The

Sun'/'I Get Around'/'All Summer Long'/'Little Honda'/'Wendy'/'Don't Back Down'/'Do You Wanna Dance'/'When I Grow Up (To Be A Man)'/'Dance, Dance, Dance'/'Please Let Me Wonder'/'She Knows Me Too Well'/ 'Radio station jingles'#/'Concert promo & Hushabye'#*.

CD 2 – 'California Girls'/'Help Me Rhonda' (45 version)/'Then I Kissed Her'/'And Your Dream Comes True'/'The Little Girl I Once Knew'/'Barbara Ann' (45 edit) /'Ruby Baby'#/'KOMA jingle'#/ 'Sloop John B'/'Wouldn't It Be Nice'/ 'You Still Believe In Me'/'God Only Knows'/ 'Hang On To Your Ego'#/'I Just Wasn't Made For These Times' /'Pet Sounds'/ 'Caroline, No'/'Good Vibrations'/'Our Prayer'#/'Heroes And Villains' ("cantina" version)/'Heroes And Villains' (sections)#/ 'Wonderful'#/ 'Cabin Essence'/'Wind Chimes'#/'Heroes And Villains' (intro)#/'Do You Like Worms'# /'Vega-Tables'#/'I Love To Say Da Da'#/'Surf's Up'#/'With Me Tonight'.

CD 3 – 'Heroes And Villains'/ 'Darlin''/'Wild Honey'/'Let The Wind Blow'/'Can't Wait Too Long'#/'Cool, Cool Water'#/'Meant For You'/'Friends'/Little

Bird'/'Busy Doin' Nothin''/'Do It Again'/'I Can Hear Music'/'I Went To Sleep'/'Time To Get Alone' /'Break Away'/'Cottonfields' (45 version)/'San Miguel'/'Games Two Can Play'#/'I Just Got My Pay'#/'This Whole World'/'Add Some Music To Your Day'/'Forever'/Our Sweet Love'/'H.E.L.P. Is On The Way'#/'4th Of July'#/'Long Promised Road'/'Disney Girls'/'Surf's Up'/'Til I Die'.

CD 4 – 'Sail On Sailor'/'California Saga-California' (LP mix)/'The Trader'/'Funky Pretty'/'Fairytale Music'#/'You Need A Mess Of Help To Stand Alone'/'Marcella'/'All This Is That'/'Rock And Roll Music' (LP mix)/'It's OK'/'Had To Phone Ya'/'That Same Song'/ 'It's Over Now'#/'Still I Dream Of It'#/'Let Us Go On This Way'/'The Night Was So Young'/'I'll Bet He's Nice'/'Airplane'/ 'Come Go With Me'/'Our Team'#/'Baby Blue'/ 'Good Timin''/'Goin' On'/'Getcha Back'/ 'Kokomo'.

CD 5 (all tracks unreleased except #) – 'In My Room' (demo)/'Radio Spot 1'/'I Get Around' track/'Radio Spot 2'/'Dance, Dance, Dance' track/'Hang On To Your Ego' session/'God Only Knows' session/'Good Vibrations' sessions#/'Heroes And Villains'

track/'Cabin Essence' track/'Surf's Up' track/'Radio Spot 3'/'All Summer Long' (vocals/track)/'Wendy' (v/t)/'Hushabye' (v/t)/'When I Grow Up (To Be A Man)' (v/t)/'Wouldn't It Be Nice' (v/t)/'California Girls' (vocals)/'Radio Spot 4' /'Concert intro-Surfin' USA'*/'Surfer Girl'* /'Be True To Your School'*/'Good Vibrations'*/'Surfer Girl'*.

(Note: the original UK release of the boxed set included a [dubious] 6th 'bonus' CD containing the following tracks: 'Bluebirds Over The Mountain'/'Tears In The Morning'/'Here Comes The Night' (12" disco version)/'Lady Lynda'/'Sumahama'. Evidently the work of some bright spark at EMI.)

The titles discussed below are solely those not covered in the main text of this volume... even so, the number of additions to The Beach Boys (legally) released legacy is impressive.

LITTLE SURFER GIRL
(B.Wilson)

Tentatively dating from late 1962/early 1963 (the Bob referred to is Bob Norberg, with whom Brian Wilson shared an apartment at

this time), this sorely incomplete fragment hints at Brian's romantic tendencies.

PUNCHLINE
(B.Wilson)

The organ riff in this otherwise undistinguished instrumental – recorded in January 1963 – re-emerged in 'Surfin USA'. The forced laughter underlines the title in truly heavy-handed fashion.

THINGS WE DID LAST SUMMER
(Styne/Cahn)

Brian Wilson recalls that this Four Freshmen-styled item was recorded for a film whose title is now lost forever. Murry Wilson would have loved this vocal antique, recorded in 1963.

RUBY BABY
(Leiber/Stoller)

This 'Party!' out-take finds Brian Wilson in fine voice (and oinks...).

GAMES TWO CAN PLAY
(B.Wilson)

Recorded during the 'Add Some Music'/ 'Sunflower' sessions, this neat little 'day-in-the-life' song from Brian Wilson features a somewhat sparse arrangement and production, redeemed by some thoroughly good humoured (and accurate) lyrics.

I JUST GOT MY PAY
(B.Wilson/Love)

A familiar title on the collector's circuit, this prototype for 'Marcella' hails from the same era as the previous entry, and similarly boasts a spartan feel. Love weighs in with a fine vocal.

H.E.L.P. IS ON THE WAY
(B.Wilson/Love)

Recorded in the period between 'Sunflower' and 'Surf's Up', this tongue in cheek ode to health food is maybe a little too preachy for its own good, but wholesome fun nonetheless, sporting fine group harmonies, and some of the daftest lyrics Love has ever penned.

4TH OF JULY
(D.Wilson/Rieley)

A 'Surf's Up' discard, Dennis Wilson's typically dense track is accompanied by some similarly opaque lyrics from Jack Rieley which, according to their author, dealt with the controversy surrounding the government's attempt to suppress the *New York Times*. Quite. Although credited as a Brian Wilson production, it sounds much more like the work of Dennis.

IT'S OVER NOW
(B.Wilson)

Both this melancholy ballad and the following track date from Brian Wilson's post-'15 Big Ones' burst of creativity (and both feature string and horn arrangements by Dick Reynolds). Brian, with brother Carl and then-wife Marilyn, offer up another glimpse into his heart and soul (seemingly a desolate terrain...). Brian wrote this for Frank Sinatra, from whom no reply ever came. The strange timbre of Carl Wilson's voice has been ascribed to a tape-speed fault... but strangely, neither Brian nor Marilyn are similarly affected.

STILL I DREAM OF IT
(B.Wilson)

Another ballad, fairly dripping with wry resignation and lifted into the classic category by a wonderfully homespun lyric and delivery from Brian Wilson. Tremendously affecting.

OUR TEAM
(B.Wilson/C.Wilson/D.Wilson/Jardine/Love)

An outcast from the 'M.I.U. Album' sessions, this mildly amusing celebration of team spirit (ironic, considering the prevailing situation during the recordings) features just about everybody at the Maharishi International University chipping in behind Alan Jardine and Brian Wilson.

FLOTSAM AND JETSAM

Given the sheer size of The Beach Boys back catalogue and their longevity as a recording act, it's hardly surprising that there are a number of recordings as yet unavailable on commercial CD. These are listed below, in chronological order, purely for the sake of completeness.

'What'd I Say' (Charles)
'Beach Boys/Brian Wilson Rarities' (Capitol ST 26463 Australia): A live recording from a 1964 Sydney concert.

'Why Do Fools Fall In Love' (45 mix)
The B-side of 'Fun, Fun, Fun'.

'Susie Cincinnati' (45 mixes)
The B-side of both 'Add Some Music To Your Day' and 'Child of Winter', each a different mono mix.

'Cuddle Up' (45 mix)
The B-side of the 'Mess Of Help' single.

'Child Of Winter' (B.Wilson/Kalinich)
Bother-Reprise RPS 1321: the 1974 Xmas
single.

'Honkin' Down The Highway'
'Beach Boys Love You': complete with drum
intro.

'Peggy Sue'/'Winds Of Change'
'M.I.U. Album': the correct mixes.

'It's A Beautiful Day'
Soundtrack LP (Lorimar JS 36174): the
unedited version.

'California Dreaming'
'Rock 'n' Roll City' cassette (Radio Shack 51-
3009): the original mix.

'Chasin' The Sky' (Proffer)
Up The Creek soundtrack LP (Pasha SZ
39333)

'East Meets West' (Gaudio)
FBI 7701 45, performed with The Four
Seasons.

'Rock 'n' Roll To The Rescue'
12" Capitol 15234 45: instrumental and 'per-
cadella' mixes.

'Fourth Of July, A Rockin' Celebration Of
America' LP (Love Foundation): live perfor-
mances with… Ringo Starr - 'Back In The
USSR' (Lennon/McCartney); The Oak Ridge
Boys - 'Come Go With Me'; Julio Iglesias -
'Surfer Girl'; Jimmy Page & Friends – 'Barbara
Ann'.

'Runaway' (Shannon)
'25 Years Of Good Vibrations' LP (Brother
Records SL-9431): a live version recorded in
Cleveland, 1981.

'Happy Endings' (Johnston)
Critique 7-99392 45, performed with Little
Richard.

'California Girls'
The B-side of the preceding title, and a live
recording.

'Problem Child' (Melcher)
RCA 2546-4 cassette single.

In addition to the currently unavailable songs listed above, there are a handful of recordings – none of any great significance – scattered across odd albums and CD singles. These are briefly dealt with here.

'Celebration' (LP Ode SPX 7008 – released January 1971: CD Sequel NEX CD 145): this live album from the 1970 Big Sur Festival at Monterey includes an excellent version of 'Wouldn't It Be Nice'.

CD Single Capitol CDLC 549 (UK released 1989) the tracks are 'Still Cruisin''/'Kokomo'/'Rock 'n' Roll To The Rescue' (Beach Party extended mix)/'Lady Liberty'.

CD Single Capitol 552-20 3642 3 (Europe 1989) - tracks are 'California Dreamin' (version 2)/'Kokomo' (Spanish version)/'Wipe Out' (with the Fat Boys).

'Two Rooms' Celebrating The Songs Of Elton John & Bernie Taupin (LP Mercury 845 749-1, CD Mercury 845 749-2 – released 1991). The Beach Boys contribution to this various artists tribute album was 'Crocodile Rock'. Produced by Gus Dudgeon and with leads from Carl & Alan (and no involvement from Brian), this is one of the lesser moments of the set, being resolutely uninspiring.

INDEX